DATE DUE			

More Blue Ribbon Science Fair Projects

Other Books by Maxine Iritz
Blue Ribbon Science Fair Projects
Super Science Fair Sourcebook
Science Fair: Developing a Successful and Fun Project
Winning the Grand Award: Successful Strategies for the ISEF Competition

More Blue Ribbon Science Fair Projects

Maxine Iritz

McGraw-Hill

New York   San Francisco   Washington, D.C.   Auckland   Bogotá
Caracas   Lisbon   London   Madrid   Mexico City   Milan
Montreal   New Delhi   San Juan   Singapore
Sydney   Tokyo   Toronto

Library of Congress Cataloging-in-Publication Data

Iritz, Maxine.
    More blue ribbon science fair projects / Maxine Iritz.
      p. cm.
    includes index.
    Summary: Discusses the organization and development of school science projects from their beginnings as vague concepts, to the experiment and testing stages, and finally to completion and display.
    ISBN 0-07-134668-6 (acid-free paper)
    1. Science projects—Juvenile literature. [1. Science projects.] I. Title.

Q182.3 .I7516 1999
507'.8—dc21
99-048586

McGraw-Hill

A Division of The McGraw·Hill Companies

1 2 3 4 5 6 7 8 9 0   QPD/QPD   9 0 9 8 7 6 5 4 3 2 1 0 9

ISBN 0-07-134668-6

This book was designed, edited, and set in Garamond and Perky by TopDesk Publishers' Group. *Printed and bound by* Quebecor/Dubuque.

McGraw-Hill books are available at special quantity discounts to use as premiums and sales promotions, or for use in corporate training programs. For more information, please write to the Director of Special Sales, McGraw-Hill, 11 West 19th Street, New York, NY 10011. Or Contact your local bookstore.

 This book is printed on recycled, acid-free paper containing a minimum of 50% recycled, de-inked fiber.

Contents

Introduction

Welcome to *More Blue Ribbon Science Fair Projects.* This new edition is designed to give you all the tools that you'll need to do a successful project and have a great time doing it. You've probably never done anything like this before, but this book was written especially for you, students who are starting their very first science projects.

As with anything else, doing a project is both good news and bad news. The bad news is that you're probably worried about how you'll ever manage to do it. For most of you, a science project is a larger and more complex piece of work than you've ever done.

The good news is that you already have many of the skills you'll need to finish a project. Even if you don't picture yourself as a budding scientist, you'll see that a lot of the abilities you do have will come in very handy. Do you like to write? The research paper will give you a place to use and display your talents. If you're an artist in the making, just wait until you start designing and building your project display. An amateur detective? Research was made for you. And if you're crazy about details, lists, and statistics, I know you'll keep an excellent log of your experiment. Even better news—some of you will be discovering these special talents for the first time, which will give you a great feeling of success and accomplishment.

Besides discovering these very real aptitudes and abilities for the first time, doing a science project is a great opportunity to learn something about yourself. Some of you will find that when you're under pressure, you do your best work. You'll drive your parents and teachers crazy in the process, but waiting until the last minute is your thing. Doing a science project may help you to work on a schedule—most teachers will give you mini-deadlines, for example, for your bibliography, your research paper, or your list of procedures, to keep you on track. Others will find that you don't need the stress—you'd rather do a little bit at a time and avoid the last-minute rush. You may be extremely neat and organized, or you may be happiest surrounded by papers, pens, glue, markers, computer manuals, and so on. There's no one way to be successful, but understanding how you like to work will help you to do your best.

The purpose of this book is to guide you through your science project, from choosing your topic to presenting at a science fair. Each step of the way, we'll give you the information you need, steps to follow, pitfalls to avoid, and helpful hints to overcome any obstacles that may spring up in your path. We'll follow some projects through from the beginning to the end, and we'll include many examples along the way. At the end of each chapter, there's a summary of the points that we've covered.

To make sure that this book would be helpful for the greatest number of people, we've geared it toward science fairs that follow International Science and Engineering Fair (ISEF) guidelines. However, your requirements may differ, depending on your teacher and your grade level.

The best way to use this book is to read it through once, to get the big picture of what's involved in doing a project. Then, as you begin looking for ideas, doing research, completing the experiment, and putting together the display, use each chapter as a step-by-step guide. As you do each phase of the project, review each chapter summary to make sure that you've covered all the bases.

To help you along, we've also included a Science Project Organizer in Appendix A. Using these forms and checklists will help you to make sure that you've thought of everything. Remember, though, that these forms and lists are fairly general—if they don't apply to the way your project is set up, you may want to change them to suit your needs. If you're using a computer, you may want to duplicate, and maybe modify, them on disk. As you use the forms, jot down your ideas and observations in the margins, underline, make notes—in other words, make it a science project workbook. And who knows— in a few years, a younger sister or cousin may thank you for it.

You certainly don't need a computer to do a successful science project, but we'll supply plenty of computer tips to show how you can take advantage of the technology to help you.

Theresa Bishop, whose two projects are featured throughout this book, is a great example of what, beyond science, you can gain from doing a project. "It has brought our family even closer together," she said. "Even though they insisted I do the work myself, my projects have become family projects." From finding out all they could about a topic to building and testing the models that she would use in her experiments, the rest of the family has joined in. They've also developed a new way of looking at the world. "Wherever we go," said Mrs. Bishop, "we see things that make us ask questions. And questions are at the heart of a science project." Theresa has also learned a few useful, everyday skills—building her models has helped her learn her way around the workshop—she now knows how to use power tools!

You may wonder what all this has to do with you, anyway. You don't even like science. Take it from the words of a student who did three successful projects and then went on to college. In his first semester, his class was assigned a large research project in sociology class. Many of his classmates were in a panic, but this young man remained calm. "Just another science project," he said with a smile.

And saving the best news for last, you may actually find that the entire experience is fun!

Chapter 1

Choosing a Topic

Okay, you may be thinking—it's all very well to talk about how much fun this is going to be, but I don't even know what my project's going to be about. Finding a topic is the first, may be the hardest, and is certainly the most important part of the whole science project experience. You need to find something that's interesting and fun, a topic for which you can find enough information, and one where you'll be able to do the experiment with the resources that you have available.

In talking to many students around the country, I've found that the ones who are most successful and enjoy their projects the most are the ones who work on something that they like. It's the difference between having fun and doing a long, boring, difficult assignment. Thinking about science, many of you may wonder what it could possibly have to do with the things that you enjoy in your real life, but take a look at some of these project ideas.

From the wonderful world of sports, many students have come up with some really great project ideas:

✓ Is there a home field advantage in sports?
✓ Do tennis balls bounce differently on clay or grass courts?
✓ Which swimsuit material has the least drag?
✓ Are the best baseball bats wood or aluminum?
✓ What is the best angle for taking a shot on goal?

As you can see, if sports are your thing, there's a world of ideas out there. If you can always rattle off all the statistics for your favorite team, you may want to do a mathematics project. Physics (now don't moan, it's not as hard as it sounds) is the home for projects about the motion of a ball or a hockey puck. Have you wondered why a piece of sports equipment was designed the way it was, and thought there was a better way? Maybe an engineering project is for you.

You may want to do a project about some everyday products. Science project time has turned many homes into mini consumer testing labs. New and improved? Whiter and brighter? How about those nutritional facts? Science is not only about the discoveries of tomorrow, it is everyday life, here and now.

✓ Cool it Orville Redenbacher—Does frozen popcorn pop better?

✓ Do certain household items help prevent rust?

✓ Out of nine selected woods, which absorbs the most water?

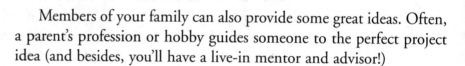

Members of your family can also provide some great ideas. Often, a parent's profession or hobby guides someone to the perfect project idea (and besides, you'll have a live-in mentor and advisor!)

✓ Do cars follow too closely? (Dad investigates accidents for the DMV.)

✓ Is San Diego County endangered by acid rain? (Mom's a statistician and Grandpa's a professor of environmental science.)

✓ Does Involuntary smoking cause decreased lung capacity? (Dad's an MD.)

✓ Why do plants grow up? (Mom has a green thumb.)

Another place to look for ideas is in your own life. What kinds of things are important to you and your friends?

✓ Stuck on You—the effects of different substances on dental adhesives. (I hate giving up sodas while my braces are on.)

✓ The influence of favorite color, sex, age, hair, and eye color on wardrobe choices. (I need new clothes.)

✓ Do color and smell influence taste? (How about that weird blue food?)

✓ The effect of watching TV on test scores. (I can *too* do my homework while I watch MTV.)

✓ Is too much sugar and fat bad for you? (But they taste so good.)

As you can see, your science project does not have to be solemn. You can do a project on just about anything, as long as you follow the scientific method as you do your experiment (but more about that later).

You'll notice that I said "just about" anything. Yes, there are some things that are better avoided, and here are a few: Topics that have been done, redone, and overdone, year after year, are best avoided. If you get copies of science project programs from previous years, you'll quickly see what some of these are. Also, if you tell your teacher your project idea and she groans or gets a painful expression on her face, you'll know that she's seen far too many plants potted in coffee grinds. However, if you can put a new twist on an old topic, it may be just the thing.

Another thing to avoid is a topic that requires experimenting on live vertebrates. Besides being a lot of work, there are many rules about experimenting on animals. You'll need a special advisor to make sure that the animals are properly and humanely cared for, and you'll have to get approvals for any work that you do. If you want to do work with animals, consider invertebrates or projects that do not involve invasive experimentation.

✓ Which sugar substance do ants prefer?
✓ The Canine Allergy-Obesity Connection
✓ The Efficiency of Various Horse Shampoos
✓ A Comparison of Ocean and Bay Plankton

Another thing you'll want to avoid is a project that simply builds a model (believe me, teachers have seen more model volcanoes and solar systems than they can count). However, this doesn't rule out building a model to use in your experiment, or building a "better mousetrap" as an engineering project.

Although we're not yet at the stage of planning the project in detail, once you find an idea, you'll want to make sure that you'll be able to follow through on the project. Here are some questions to ask yourself

✓ Is there enough information about this topic? A visit to the library or a search on the Internet will let you know what's available. Check out the chapter on doing project research for more information on finding sources.
✓ What will I need to do my experiment? Is the equipment available? If not, can I build it myself?
✓ How much will it cost? Your parents may be helpful here, getting prices, and also deciding whether they can help with expenses.
✓ Is it okay with my parents? Can I use the guest room for my exper-

iment for the next three months? Can I keep the earthworms in the bathroom sink?

✓ Will it be safe? If you're using electricity or chemicals, you and your parents might need to check this one out together.

✓ Do I have enough experience to do this particular project? Although the purpose of doing a project is to learn new things, now is not the time to take on something you know absolutely nothing about. Even if you have an expert in your family, remember that this is *your* project, not your Mom's or Dad's.

✓ Is there enough time to do the experiment? Usually, you'll have 3 or 4 months to do the entire project, so don't plan an experiment using a shrub that takes a year to grow.

If you plan to take your project to a science fair, it will be classified into one of the International Science and Engineering Fair (ISEF) categories. To see where your idea falls (or to get some ideas) check the list of categories in Appendix B.

Of course, your project may not wind up exactly where you thought it would. The student who did the project on dental adhesives entered it in the Medicine and Health category, only to find that was reclassified as an engineering project because it was really about the properties of adhesives and not about orthodontia.

One mistake that lots of students make at this stage is biting off more than they can chew. Remember that as much as you'd like to, you're not going to find a cure for cancer doing your science project. You may, however, find a small piece of the topic that you have the knowledge to tackle and the time to finish.

To show how others have found project ideas, let's look at our featured projects. Sabrina Glenn looked at many of the ads on TV for batteries and wondered, "How can all of them last the longest?" From that question, she decided to do a project testing three different brands of batteries to see which in fact gave the most "juice" for the longest time.

For Theresa Bishop's experiments on wind turbines and desalinization, she found her topics by asking what if—What if we find ourselves without the energy to produce electricity, and what if some natural disaster left us without safe drinking water?

For the wind turbine project, the idea became more specific when Theresa saw illustrations of different types of windmills in a science book. Because everything is a family affair for the Bishops, part of the planning for the project was a family outing to the huge windmill farms outside Palm Springs, California. Though the weather was cold and windy (just the right conditions for generating wind power and producing electricity), the sight of the different models of windmills in action prompted Theresa to decide exactly what she wanted to accomplish with her project. In addition, she gathered some valuable information from the visitor's center in Palm Springs. The focus of the project became the testing and evaluation of various types of windmills.

Theresa's other project, about the methods of desalinating water, came out of a family trip to Santa Barbara. When her Dad got lost, they came across a desalinating plant, a plant that removes salt from water to make it drinkable. She had read that for many years desalinating has been considered as a possible freshwater source However, she was also aware that there were few active plants. As a result, she decided to actually create the devices to reproduce three different methods of desalination and look at the benefits and drawbacks of each method.

While reading this, you've probably come up with a few good ideas of your own. Jot them down and rank them, starting with your favorite. Then, ask yourself the questions listed earlier and see which idea will fly. You can use the form in the Science Project Organizer to help you check out your ideas. Once you've done that, check it out with your science teacher. He may have a few points that you haven't thought of.

Have you made your decision? Great. Let's get started.

➤ In Conclusion...

Ask yourself these questions:

Am I interested in the topic?

Can I find sources of information?

Do I have enough time to finish the project?

Can my parents help (or, at least, will they not object)?

Can I find all the materials I need, and can I afford them?

Have I talked with my science teacher about my topic?

Chapter 2

Finding Background Information

Depending on your grade, school, and teacher, a background research paper may be required for a science project. "But that's worse than doing an experiment," I can hear some of you moan. There's no denying that it's a big assignment, but if you break it down into smaller pieces, it can be easier and more fun.

Why Do Research?

To do a worthwhile experiment, you first need to understand past and current theories, research, and discoveries. If your topic is very general and you're having trouble narrowing it down, checking out the information that's available may help you to focus your efforts. Your research will also help you come up with your question and hypothesis, which we'll discuss in Chapter 4.

Doing research will also help in your careers as students. As long as you're in school, you'll need to write research papers on many subjects (even some that you have absolutely no interest in). Some of these papers may be pure research, where you'll just need to gather and organize factual data. For others, you'll need to learn the facts and then interpret them, showing that you can understand and apply the facts that you've learned. In any event, you need to know how to find the data.

Tracking down information is a skill you'll use throughout your lives. As working adults, parents, or curious, informed citizens, this ability is essential. If your parents are helping you with this project, they'll know what I mean!

Once you get started, this part of your project can be fun. In many ways, it's like playing detective. You may find one source that is not especially useful but leads you to three or four other sources. As with any other mystery, your research may send you down some blind alleys, which will temporarily throw you off track. However, if you keep at it, you'll eventually find what you need. Along the way, you might learn other fascinating things, perhaps on other subjects leading to new interests (or next year's project).

Finding the Facts—A Brief Guide

The best place to start your fact-finding mission is with the sources that are closest to you. These include your textbooks and any encyclopedias or other reference materials you may have at home, or in your school library. These references may only give you the most basic information, but they will at least help you to see the different aspects of your topic. Also, the bibliographies in these volumes might point out other sources.

Computer Tip

Along with the old-fashioned 24-volume encyclopedia, you might have access to an encyclopedia on CD-ROM.

The next stop is your public library. Basically, there are two ways to find information there, through either an on-line or a card catalog system.

If your library has On-Line Public Access (OPAC) catalogs, this will help you find what's available in your area. These catalogs are also used in many colleges and universities. Some library systems may have their entire system on an OPAC, but others may only have sources later than a certain date. For earlier works, you'll need to use the card catalog.

In an OPAC, besides searching by author and title, you can find information by keyword. For example you could use the keyword "tsunami" if you wanted all information about tidal waves. Actually, you can use both "tsunami" and "tidal wave" to get a wider scope of information. Sometimes, however, you'll get more sources than you actually want to see, so you'll need to narrow the search. If you're only interested in tidal waves in Alaska during the 20th century, you can enter this information for a more specific list of references. For sources that are in the local library, you can not only get the list but you'll find out if the works are in the library, at another branch, or currently circulating.

However, if you need to use the card catalog and do not know how, ask the librarian to help you. Local branch libraries often have card catalogs that use the Dewey decimal system, while other libraries use the LC, or Library of Congress, method to catalog books. Both methods will guide you to the areas of the library where you'll find materials dealing with your subject.

Some libraries also use a microfilm or microfiche catalog. This usually shows everything available in the entire library system. If the books or articles you need are in other branches, you may be able to have them delivered to your branch. Otherwise, you'll need to travel to other parts of your city or county. Eventually, your search will probably lead you to your library's main branch to get all the information you need.

Don't think that you have to live in a big city to do research. To begin, of course, you'll have your school and local libraries. Then, all you need is a computer (or writing materials and a post office) to gather material from all over the world. However, don't limit yourself to libraries. Publications dealing with just about every conceivable area of science are available from the U.S. government. Private companies are usually very cooperative and are often willing to share information, especially with students. Even foreign governments and international organizations might be willing to send material.

For the moment, however, back to the library. Some books are available for you to borrow, but before you bring the book home, check it out to see that it really meets your needs. Check the copyright date to see if it's recent enough to have the most up-to-date information. In some fields, even information that is a few months old can be obsolete. Also, be sure that the material is on your level. A manuscript written for a PhD candidate in nuclear physics may be too difficult if you're a seventh grader attempting your first science project. Looking at the table of contents, index, and appendices might also give you a good idea of whether this book will be useful for you.

Other materials are classified as reference material, which means you will have to use them at the library. If you need to do that, please remember library etiquette. Keep your materials close at hand and neat, talk in whispers, and don't eat or drink on the premises. Be sure you have plenty of paper and pencils, since there's usually no place to buy anything at the library.

You can also make copies of important information to bring home. Most libraries today have photocopiers, which are most helpful. But be prepared and bring plenty of change. These machines gobble up money faster than a video arcade!

Helpful Hint

If you plan to make lots of copies, buy a copier card. This works somewhat like a bus pass, since you prepay the cost of making a number of copies on the library's machine. You can also use the card for copying material from microfiche or the library's computer.

Don't limit your research to books. There's a lot of valuable information in newspapers and popular magazines, such as *Newsweek, Time,* and *Readers Digest.* There are also magazines that popularize scientific subjects, such as *Science Digest, National Geographic, Today's Health,* or *Psychology Today.* Finally, look into specialized, scholarly periodicals that deal specifically with the field you're interested in. To find these types of articles, use a periodical index, such as *The Readers Guide to Periodic Literature.*

If you need a recent newspaper or magazine, the library will usually have the actual issue on hand. Older issues will probably be available on microfilm or microfiche. The microfiche reader may have a copier attached (which takes the copier card as well as nickels, dimes, and quarters) so that you can make copies of important pages. You can also get the actual articles from the computer and print out the articles that you need. Again, the printouts aren't free, so have your coins or copier card handy.

College and university libraries often will have books and periodicals that a public library does not carry, especially if the college is famous for a particular area of science. The people who work there, who are sometimes students, can be very helpful in guiding you to the facilities available. If a conveniently located university library has a lot of useful information for you, see if you can buy a library card. This gives you the same library privileges as the college or university students.

Institutes and foundations usually function the same way as university libraries. Without special access, you can't take the materials out of the building (there are copiers here too)! However, these can be extremely good sources of specialized information, and may lead you to experts in your field.

One of the most extensive sources of information is the U.S. Government, our nation's largest publisher. You can find government references that would be helpful by looking at the U.S. government departments and agencies that publish material that you may need. In your search, don't only look in the obvious places. The Department of Commerce, for example, has an annual publication titled *United States Earthquakes*, and the Department of the Treasury, which is in charge of Alcohol and Tobacco, has many publications on those subjects. Usually, you can buy some government publications from the appropriate agency, but allow enough time to receive the materials you order. Many a project has stumbled waiting for an order to be processed.

Branches of the military service, corporations and professional associations are also excellent sources of information on a variety of scientific and engineering topics. Often, they publish pamphlets that are yours for the asking!

For the project on Wind Turbines, Theresa Bishop used a variety of sources, including encyclopedias, science textbooks, Internet sites, government publications, and periodicals, such as *Popular Mechanics* magazine. Her research focused mainly on the history of windmills, as well as on the history and sources of electricity.

As you look for your sources of information, review the checklist in the Science Project Organizer in Appendix A, to be sure you've left no stone unturned!

Taking Notes and Sample Bibliography Formats

Now that you've found your sources, it's time to choose the information you'll use for your background research paper. Since every fact you use will come from one of your sources, the first task is to start your bibliography. Examples of standard bibliography formats are shown next.

Periodical

Patrick Huygne, "Earthquakes, the Solar Connection," *Science Digest,* XC (October 1982), 73-75.

Interview

Dr. J. Holman III, Orthodontist, Interview, 11/23/89.

Books

By single author

Lauber, Patricia, *Of Man and Mouse,* New York, Viking Press, 1971.

By multiple authors

Anderson, Garron P., S. John Bennett, and Lawrence K. DeVries, *Analysis and Testing of Adhesive Bonds,* Long Beach, CA, Foster Publishing Co., 1971.

Encyclopedias

Selection without author

"Galena," Encyclopedia International, 1974.

Selection with author

Roderick, Thomas H., "Gene," *Encyclopedia International,* 1974.

Government or other institutional publication

Science Service, ABSTRACTS; 38TH International Science and Engineering Fair, Washington, DC, 1987.

When you take notes, select only the information that directly relates to your subject. If you find the same facts in several sources, use the presentation that makes the most sense to you. Record each fact, *in your own words.* Whether you use index cards, a notebook, your word processor, or a data base to "write down" the information, it's important to use *your own words.* This will help you understand and absorb the material. Code each fact to show the source, including the page number. If it's important to quote the material word for word, be sure to use quotation marks. To help you take notes efficiently, you may want to use the following checklist and form. There's also another copy in the science project organizer, which you can copy and take with you to the library.

Name the source.

Author: _____

Title: _____

Publisher: _____

City: _____

Date: _____

Pages: _____

Write a summary. Jot down the main ideas or opinions in one or two summary sentences.

_____

_____

_____

_____

_____

_____

_____

List the important details. List specific facts that support the main ideas. Make sure to use quotation marks if you're using direct quotes.

_____

_____

_____

_____

_____

_____

_____

_____

➤ **In Conclusion...**

Have I looked for books and periodicals in the libraries, government publications, experts in the field, and on the Internet?

Have I started a working bibliography?

Did I take notes in my own words?

If I'm using quotes, did I make sure to copy the information word for word and note the source?

Writing the Background Research Paper

Now that you've gathered your information, it's time to tackle the research paper.

Why Do a Paper?

Perhaps it will be easier for you to begin this part of the project if you understand why it is necessary and how much effort is required. The size and scope of the research paper will depend on your teacher's requirements. Sometimes, a simple review of the literature is all that's needed, while other teachers want a large paper. Regardless of how long or involved your paper will be, there are some basic elements.

Outlining

Before you begin the actual writing, review all your facts and try to find a few themes, or main topics. Then, find the subtopics that will be grouped underneath the main headings.

Write down, in outline form, what you want to say in your background research paper. If you are not well acquainted with using outline form, it is

Introduction:
I.   The first subtopic
   A. First supporting information or detail for the subtopic
   B. Second supporting information or detail for the subtopic
   C. Third supporting detail or information for the subtopic

II.   The second subtopic
  A. First supporting information or detail for the subtopic
  B. Second supporting information or detail for the subtopic
  C. Third supporting detail or information for the subtopic

Computer Tip

If you've recorded your facts using a word processor, check out the automatic outlining feature.

Remember that in outline form, if an item is subdivided, it should contain at least two elements. Otherwise, the information should have been included in the division. For example,

IV.   Other insects
  A. Tarantulas

should read

IV.   Other insects; tarantulas, etc.

Once you've done the outline, it's easy to arrange your facts. Use the outline to assign all your facts into one of the topics or subtopics.

Don't worry if you have a few facts that don't seem to belong anywhere. They may be facts that don't relate to your subject, or you may find that you need to include another topic or subtopic in your outline.

Review the following outline of an outline to help you do your own outline.

Organization

- The introduction states the main topic or idea of the outline.
- Each paragraph in your paper has a subtopic.
- Each subtopic describes the main idea for a paragraph.
- Supporting information and details for a subtopic are listed under the subtopic.
- Each piece of supporting information is listed separately.
- When supporting information is listed under a subtopic, there are at least two pieces of information in the list. If there is only one piece of information to support a subtopic, the information is included in the subtopic.
- The conclusion summarizes the main idea of the outline.

Format

- For a sentence outline:
  Each outline entry is a complete sentence with a period at the end of the sentence.

- For a topic outline:
  Each outline entry is a phrase with no punctuation at the end of the phrase.

Spelling

- All words are spelled correctly.
- All typing errors are corrected.

Helpful Hint

Don't discard these facts just because you don't think they belong in your paper. This information may be important later, as you do your experiment. Also, if you build on your project next year, they may be useful then.

Next, arrange the facts in each topic or subtopic into a logical sequence. These sequenced facts will become the basis of the first draft of your paper. I'm sure you already know how long the paper should be, so you can check your outline to see if you have enough information for the paper. If not, back to the library! If your outline has too many points to cover in the amount of pages you need, you'll have to shorten the outline, either by cutting out certain points or by cutting down on the number of facts under each point.

Writing the Paper

The first few paragraphs should introduce the topic you're writing about and the experiment you'll do. Then, follow your outline to show you exactly what to write next. The last several paragraphs should summarize the facts you've discussed, and finally, you should predict what you believe your experiment will prove. In short, tell them what you're going to say, say it, and tell them what you've just said.

Computer Tip

If you recorded your facts using a data base or word processor, use your software to arrange the facts in the proper sequence. Delete any unrelated information and store your file under a new name, just in case.

If you wrote down all your facts in your own words, you'll find it easier to write an original research paper. Remember, though, that a paper is not just a bunch of facts strung together. Your teachers, as well as science fair judges, will look for continuity, creativity, and educated interpretation of the facts. Ultimately, the paper should relate to your proposed experiment.

One valuable resource on writing is Strunk & White's *Elements of Style*. Originally published in 1919, this small, inexpensive paperback is one you can use throughout your student career. In fact, your English teacher may require you to use it. The book describes rules of correct grammar, teaches you to write clearly, and shows you how to avoid common writing mistakes.

As you develop your paper, which clearly has a beginning, a middle, and an end, you will realize that the paper is made of several paragraphs. In fact, you can think of each paragraph as a mini-paper, since each one also has a beginning, a middle, and an end. (Remember, *"Tell them what you're going to say, say it, and tell them what you've just said!"*) To help you develop each paragraph, or mini-paper, use these guidelines.

Write a topic sentence. What is the main idea of your paragraph?

_____

_____

_____

_____

_____

_____

List important details. What facts do you want to include in your paragraph to support your idea?

_____

_____

_____

_____

_____

_____

_____

_____

_____

Write your paragraph. In the paragraph, write several sentences to explain, explore, and describe the idea in your topic sentence. Be sure to include all the facts that you listed.

_____

_____

_____

_____

_____

_____

_____

_____

_____

_____

Credit Your Sources

If you use someone else's words or ideas, you have to state where the ideas or words come from. To put it simply, if you use an author's exact words, be sure to put them in quotes, for example, as Mr. XY says in his book titled *Food for Surfers,* "as long as you stay away from spam, you'll stay healthy." If you don't use an exact quote but very closely paraphrase the author, you could say

Mr. XY tells us in *Food for Surfers* that to stay healthy, you should avoid spam.

Another way of crediting the author is by using a footnote. You could state in your paper: As long as you don't touch the spam, you'll be a healthy surfer.[1] A footnote, numbered 1, citing Mr. XY's book would appear on the bottom of the page. Just as with a bibliography, footnotes follow a specified format:

For the first footnoted reference to a book:

[2]Robert W. McLuggage, *A History of the American Dental Association,* (Chicago, American Dental Association, 1959), p. 475.

For subsequent references:

[4]McLuggage, pp. 33-36.

For a periodical:

[7]*Psychology Today,* October 1995, p. 47.

Using someone else's material without crediting them is called plagiarism, and as you go on in your studies, you'll realize that it's a serious offense, so get in the habit of crediting your sources.

Computer Tip

Many word processors have a feature that will keep track of your footnotes for you!

Write and Rewrite

Your rough draft is the first stab at your research paper. There are no rules about how many drafts you should write, but each draft is an opportunity to correct, revise, rearrange, and reword the paper. You may want to type or print your early drafts with triple spacing to give yourself enough room to write in comments, ideas, or corrections. The best way to edit your drafts is to read and reread your paper (and maybe have family and friends review it too). Although they may not be scientists or writers, they can find spelling errors, awkward grammar, or badly worded sentences that you don't spot.

Computer Tip

If your word processor includes a spell checker, run it each time you create a new draft. Whenever you add new material, you may be adding misspelled words! Remember, though, that a spell checker won't catch everything. "*Their* are many species of insects" looks fine to a spell checker. However, if you also have a grammar checker, it will tell you if you put the wrong "their" there.

When you feel that your paper is the best that it can be, you are ready to create your final copy. If your drafts have been handwritten, try to borrow a typewriter or computer. Even if your handwriting is good, your teacher will appreciate seeing typed copy, and it will certainly make a good impression on science fair judges.

Regardless of how it was created, be sure your margins are correct, your text is double spaced, your name is on the paper, and you have obeyed any formatting rules your teachers have given you. Remember to include your footnotes and bibliography at the end of the report.

Now that this phase of the project is complete, make extra copies of everything. This is your insurance policy.

Computer Tip

If your files are on your hard drive, copy everything to a diskette. Be sure to include the notes, bibliography, and footnotes, as well as the final research paper. There's almost nothing more frustrating than losing long hours of research and writing from a power failure or computer crash. *Always* back up your computer files.

➤ In Conclusion...

Have I organized my facts into four or five main topics?

Did I use the proper outline form?

Have I credited all my sources and used the proper form when including exact quotations?

Did I create a draft of my paper and edit it several times?

Did I check my spelling and grammar?

Do I have backup copies of everything?

Chapter 4

Using the Scientific Method

Let's talk about what a science project actually consists of. What you'll be doing is using the scientific method to answer a question and prove a hypothesis. Actually, this is not just about your project but what science is all about—trying to solve a problem or answer a question.

Let's take a look at some of the questions you might try to answer with your project. Looking back at some of the project ideas in Chapter 1, these might be some of the questions:

- Do tennis balls bounce higher on a clay court?
- Does second-hand smoke affect breathing?
- Do students who watch more than three hours of TV get lower grades?
- Can you hit a baseball farther with a aluminum bat?
- Is the new improved detergent better than the old one?

In her project on Wind Turbines, Theresa Bishop's question was "Which type of propeller on a Wind Turbine will produce the most electricity?" In her project, Sabrina Glenn asked, "Which battery lasts the longest?"

Okay, you get the idea. The objective of all science is to answer a question or solve a specific problem. When you decide on your question, remember the word specific. Narrow down your question. For example,

> *Do students exposed to second-hand smoke have less lung capacity than those who are not exposed to second-hand smoke?*

What is the difference in distance between a baseball hit with a wood or an aluminum bat?

One of the most common mistakes that students make on their first project is to make their question too vague. You'll find it much easier to do your project if you know exactly what you want to find out.

Now that you've asked the question, what do you think that the answer will be? Decide that, and you'll have your hypothesis, which is your prediction of the outcome. In other words, the hypothesis is what you think that your project will prove. Let's look at the hypotheses created from the questions asked earlier:

I believe that students exposed to second-hand smoke have less lung capacity than students who are not exposed to second-hand smoke.

I do not believe that tennis balls bounce higher on a clay court.

I do not believe that students who watch more than three hours of TV get lower grades.

I believe you can hit a baseball 25% further with an aluminum bat.

I believe the new improved detergent works the same as the old one.

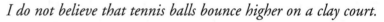

The hypothesis of the wind turbine project was:

I believe that a wind turbine with more blades will produce more electricity. I also believe that the weight and size of the blades may also affect how much energy is produced.

The hypothesis for the water desalination project was:

I believe that the distillation method of desalination will produce the most fresh water.

Now, you're almost ready to start *doing the project!* Because the heart of your science project is the experiment, it must be carefully planned and carried out to be effective and successful. Science fair judges agree that the most important factor in rating your entire project is that you follow proper scientific practices.

The scientific method is an organized way of doing an experiment, including collecting, measuring, and documenting the data. If applicable, it must include a specified variable and control, at least one experimental group, and perhaps a control group. For valid results, you must use a large enough number of samples, or perform enough tests, to make sure that what happens is not pure coincidence.

Before getting down to brass tacks, let's define some important terms.

The Subject

The goal of an experiment is to test and examine the effect of a change in environment or condition. You must choose a specific subject, one or more variables, and project controls. If, for example, you're measuring the growth of plants, the plants are the *subjects* of the experiment. In a project on how wood absorbs water, the *subjects* are the types of wood. In the project about how far you can hit a baseball with different types of bats, the baseball bats are the *subjects* of the experiment.

Variables

Many experiments use variables. An *experimental* or *independent* variable is what you will change during your experiment. For example, in the project about the effect of court surfaces on tennis balls, the three types of courts are the variables.

Another type of variable is the *measured* or *dependent variable.* This is what you will be evaluating and measuring with your experiment, such as the lung capacity of each student tested.

Controls

To make sure that your experiment is valid, you'll need to make sure that no unpredictable changes affect the experiment. *Controls,* or *controlled variables,* are the factors that must be the same for all samples in your experiment, every time that you do your experiment. This is important, because if the conditions are different, it will be impossible to know what caused the results. For example, if you're testing the effects of caffeine on different groups of goldfish, the amount and type of food given to each group, as well as the available lighting and size of each tank, must be identical. Otherwise, at the end of the experiment, it will be impossible to prove whether differences in the groups were caused by varying amounts of caffeine or the differences in diet or lighting.

Experimental and Control Groups

To draw a conclusion, you may need to compare the results of your experiment (applying the variable to your subject) with the normal condition of your subject (without making any changes). To make this type of comparison, you'll need to divide your subjects into at least two groups, the *experimental group* and the *control group.*

The *experimental group* contains of a number of subjects to which you apply the *experimental variable.* To make sure that your experiment is valid, apply these guidelines:

1. If you have several independent variables, apply one at a time, so that you'll be sure exactly what caused your results. You can also apply multiple variables by using multiple experimental groups. For example, an experiment that measured residual smoke from four cigarette brands used four experimental groups. Another project that measured the affects of second-hand smoke also had four groups: children of smokers and children of nonsmokers, both equally divided into male and female subjects.

2. It is also very important that the subjects in each experimental group be identical. For example, in a project on peripheral vision, each group contained students with the same type of vision.

3. To prevent the project from becoming too complicated, restrict the number of variables and experimental groups. Limiting the factors you're changing, will make your project easier, from your preparation to your procedures and recordkeeping, as well as the project notebook and display.

The *control group* is identical to the experimental groups, but with no variables applied. Except for not applying the variable, it must be *exactly* like the other group(s). Otherwise, there is no basis for comparison and your results may be invalid. For example, if you are testing the effect of crushed bone meal added to the soil for tomato plants, your control group would consist of a group of tomato plants that did not have bone meal added to the soil.

The sizes of the experimental and control groups are also important to the success of your project. You must have a large enough group to allow you to collect sufficient data. Your results will be more reliable if they happened to five subjects than to two, and will be just about conclusive if your sample size was ten. At the same time, you'll want to limit the number of elements to those you can adequately manage.

Another reason for having enough samples is to include a number of extras, just in case. In case what? The dog ate it, the baby knocked it over, someone threw it away, or it just plain disappeared. When dealing with plants, you'll need an even larger sample size. If you're planting seedlings, start with at least 50, and preferably more, to account for the fact that many will not sprout or may later die.

When using human responses to a survey or questionnaire, have enough to make sure that your results are representative. For surveys, any sample that is smaller than 100 is too small. In fact, when you give out a survey, it's a good idea to distribute many more than you need, to make up for those who throw away your survey or don't have time to fill it out.

You'll also have to do your experiment enough times to give conclusive results. Statistically, you can draw no conclusions based on too few trials. You'll need a *minimum* of five trials to prove a hypothesis, and even five trials would only be conclusive if they all gave the same result. To be on the safe side, plan for a minimum of ten trials.

It is important to know exactly which factors will be changed and which will remain unchanged. You may not use all these factors, depending on your hypothesis. If, for example, you were comparing the growth in plants with different drainage, your experimental variable would be the amount of drainage in each group of plants and the measured variable would be the amount of growth in each group of plants. The experimental groups might be plants with no drainage holes, plants with two drainage holes, and plants with four drainage holds. There is no control group for this experiment, but there are controls. Each group of plants will be in the same type and amount of soil, and get the same amount of water and sunlight.

Let's take a look at the hypotheses, groups, variables, and controls for several projects.

1. Hypothesis: Sandy soil erodes faster than sod.

Experimental Groups	Control Group	Variables	Controls
• California sod • California soil • California topsoil • Ohio farm soil • Virginia clay	None	Experimental • Soil samples Measured • Weight of soil samples	Amount and rate of water given for each sample

2. Hypothesis: Popcorn pops better at room temperature.

Experimental Groups	Control Group	Variables	Controls
Frozen popcorn	Room temperature popcorn	Experimental • Temperature of popcorn Measured • Number of popped kernels • Number of unpopped kernels	• Popping time • Popping method • Type of pop corn

3. Hypothesis: A moderate rate of drainage promotes plant growth.

Experimental Groups	Control Group	Variables	Controls
• Plants with 2 drainage holes • Plants with 4 drainage holes • Plants with 6 drainage holes	None	Experimental • Drainage holes Measured • Growth of plants	• Amount of water • Amount of sunlight • Type and amount of soil

4. Hypothesis: Children of smokers will have less lung capacity than children of nonsmokers.

Experimental Groups	Control Group	Variables	Controls
Students whose parents are smokers (exposed to smoke for at least 7 years)	Students whose parents are nonsmokers	Experimental • Whether parents smoked Measured • Lung capacity	• Room temperature between 72° and 80° F • Subjects free of respiratory disease or allergy

5. Hypothesis: In professional athletic competition, a team is more likely to win a game if the game is played at home.

Experimental Groups	Control Group	Variables	Controls
None	None	Experimental • Scores of MISL and NBA games Measured • Average home score • Average visiting score • Average winning score	Proportion of home and away games for each team

6. Hypothesis: I believe that a wind turbine with more blades will produce more electricity.

Experimental Groups	Control Group	Variables	Controls
Five models of wind turbines	None	Experimental • Number of blades • Type of blades Measured • Amount of energy produced	• Amount of wind applied to each model • Time of each trial

7. Hypothesis: I believe Energizer batteries will last the longest, because they are the most expensive.

Experimental Groups	Control Group	Variables	Controls
• Duracell • Energizer • Radio Shack	None	None	• Flashlights • Time of each trial

8. Hypothesis: I believe that the distillation method of desalination will produce the most fresh water.

Experimental Groups	Control Group	Variables	Controls
• Distillation • Freezing • Boiling	None	None	• Amount of seawater • Time of each trial

➤ In Conclusion...

Is your question specific enough?

Does the hypothesis clearly state what you hope your project will prove?

Have you listed the experimental groups and variables you will need? (To keep the project manageable, try to have no more than four of each.)

Does the experiment require a control group or controls?

Chapter 5

Doing the Experiment

It's finally time to start the experiment! By now you have probably collected all your equipment, defined your procedures, variables, and controls, and can't wait to begin.

To be successful, you'll need to follow a few important guidelines. Perform your trials on a regular schedule, and consistently record the necessary data. Understanding and following a proper scientific method will give your project credibility, regardless of whether your experiment has "worked."

Although you probably know exactly what materials you're going to use and what you'll be doing, you'll need to list your materials and your step-by-step procedures, as shown in the following examples:

Materials

1. 120 styrofoam cups
2. 240 Cherry Belle radish seeds
3. 1-cup measuring cup
4. Nail set to punch drainage holes in cups
5. Potting soil
6. 1-foot ruler

Procedures

1. Separated styrofoam cups into three groups of 10 cups.
2. Labeled each group FAST, MEDIUM, SLOW and numbered each cup in the group 1-40.
3. Punched holes in the bottom of each cup.

    - 6 in FAST
    - 4 in MEDIUM
    - 2 in SLOW

4. Into each cup placed ounces of soil, and two radish seeds, 8 ounces of soil.
5. Each week

    - Measured and recorded the height of each plant.
    - Watered each plant with ½ cup of water.

In Theresa Bishop's project on wind turbines, she did a lot of experimentation before she even began to do her experiment. She knew that she wanted to test the electrical output of several types of windmills. She also knew that she would need to apply a constant amount of wind to each (a project control) and would have to hook each one up to a galvanometer in order to measure results.

She built models of two-, three-, four-, and six-blade propellers, with different designs, using ice cream sticks, soda cans, and plastic cups. Next, she needed to make sure that she could produce enough "wind" to do her experiment. Using different types of fans, she found that some didn't produce enough breeze to turn any of the propellers. In fact, after testing, she eliminated two of her models that were too small to produce electricity. After trying several wind sources, she found that a 16-inch portable fan would be able to activate the propellers that remained in her experimental group.

Theresa's materials list contained not only purchased materials, but models that she built herself.

Materials

1. Galvanometer
2. 6-volt battery
3. Copper wire
4. 16-inch portable fan
5. Germanium diode
6. Several small nails
7. Plastic cups
8. Ice cream sticks
9. Soda cans

When you build your own materials, it's also a good idea to include procedures on how you created your equipment.

Building Procedures

1. Building the model

   a) Wound about 10 feet of uninsulated copper wire around a three-inch nail, leaving several inches at the beginning and end of the wire.

   b) Hammered three nails into a block of wood, forming a triangle.

   c) Wrapped beginning and end of wire around two small nails.

   d) Connected a germanium diode to the beginning and end of the wire. (The germanium diode keeps the current flowing in a single direction.)

   e) Glued a one-inch magnet to the head of a three-inch nail, and mounted the nail through the supports with the magnet just above the wire coil to make the shaft.

   f) Connected the galvanometer to the small nails with two wires.

   g) Connected a six-volt battery and observed the galvanometer showing that six volts of current were flowing through the circuit.

2. Building the propellers

   a) Two-blade propeller using ice cream sticks. This was too small and light to turn shaft-will not use in experiment.

   b) Two-blade propeller made from plastic cups. This was too small and light to turn shaft-will not use in experiment.

c) Four-blade propeller with round tips from aluminum soda cans, using half-inch inserts between the blades.

d) Three-blade propeller with square tips and one-inch inserts, from aluminum soda cans.

e) Two-blade propeller with tapered ends and no inserts, from aluminum soda cans.

f) Six-blade propeller with rounded tips and no inserts, made from aluminum soda cans. Four of the blades were an inch wide, and two of the blades were ³/₄ inch wide.

Once all the materials were bought, found, built, and tested, Theresa was able to conduct the entire experiment over one weekend.

Procedures

1. Attach each propeller onto the shaft.
2. Connect the battery and galvanometer to the model.
3. Turn on the 16-inch fan in front of the model.
4. Observe each model for five minutes, to determine how well each propeller turned.
5. Measure the electricity produced.

Theresa obviously likes making her own equipment, because her next project, on water desalination, also required her to be quite inventive. Besides deciding on how exactly she would perform the boiling and freezing methods, doing this project, she learned how to build a still. Building this took some time, trial, and error, because things didn't quite go according to plan on the first try. However, with her parents' help, she was finally able to get a working model.

Materials

1. Distillation
   a) Plexiglas
   b Aluminum pans
   c) 50-watt floodlight
   d) 32 oz. of seawater
   e) Clear sealant
   f) Duct tape

g) Right angle brackets
h) Baking pan
i) Four 5-oz. glass jars
2. Freezing
    a) Tupperware bowl
    b) Refrigerator/freezer
    c) 32 oz. of seawater

3. Boiling
    a) 1 cooking pan
    b) Aluminum foil
    c) Aluminum pans
    d) Stove
    e) 32 oz. of seawater
4. Nikon camera

Because she was dealing with three experimental groups that took a good amount of setup time and careful monitoring and observation, Theresa's procedures list was quite detailed. Again, she needed to do quite a bit of testing before the actual experiment started, because some of the desalination methods that she created did not work very well. She therefore had to fine-tune the way the still was built and the way she would boil the seawater before she was able to start recording results.

Procedures

1. Got 128 oz. of seawater from Glorietta Bay and stored in two Hi-C bottles.

2. Desalination
    a) Set up the model on a tilted board, using a shim to force the water down into the drain holes. Cut additional drain holes and waterways. Painted board and seawater pan with sealant.
    b) Put 32 oz. of seawater in still.
    c) Sealed still with duct tape around top covering and bottom of board.
    d) Set up 50-watt floodlight for heat to cause water to evaporate.
    e) Discovered that water was seeping into the wood and the glue was starting to melt. Built new cover of Plexiglas and restarted the process.
    f) Collected, measured, and tasted fresh water.

g) Collected and measured salt.

3. Freezing
    a) Froze 32 oz. of seawater.
    b) Each day, scraped ice off top of bowl.
    c) Each day, collected, measured, and tasted fresh water.
    d) Collected salt.

4. Boiling
    a) Tried using single pan to boil the seawater, but found that water was boiling out too fast.
    b) Restarted experiment with smaller pan inside large pan, with cover over everything.
    c) When water began to boil, turned pan on side and used smaller bowls to collect any water that dripped down.
    d) Boiled sample for 30 minutes and let cool for 30 minutes.
    e) Collected, tasted, and measured fresh water.
    f) Collected and measured salt.

Sabrina Glenn's experiment testing three brands of batteries had a fairly short and inexpensive list of materials.

Materials

1. Three flashlights
2. One four-pack each of Energizer, Duracell, and Radio Shack D-size alkaline batteries
3. Cardboard box for holder (grooves cut out to hold flashlights during experiment)

The procedures were quite straightforward as well, since the experiment called for her to leave the flashlights on while she watched to see if any of them quit.

Procedures

1. Put one battery into each flashlight.
2. Labeled each flashlight with battery brand used.
3. Turned each flashlight on at the same time.
4. Recorded time that each flashlight remained on.

When you do your experiment, there are several important factors to keep in mind.

1. Follow your list of procedures exactly.
2. Do your experiment on a regular schedule, for example every Tuesday afternoon.

If you do this, you can be sure that you're not introducing any unpredicted variables into your experiment. For example, in a project on drainage in plants, if you forget to water your plants on a regular schedule, you might change the effects of drainage on the plants.

Observation and Measurement

Another crucial factor in the success of your project is observation and documentation. Each time that you check your experiment, be sure to write down what you observe in a project log. This doesn't need to be anything formal-just the date and what you observed.

| ✓ | 11/5 | 10 plants in group A grew ¼ inch. Rest of plants in group A and all plants in groups B and C stayed the same. |
| ✓ | 11/12 | 7 plants in group A grew ½ inch. Rest of plants in group A, all plants in group B and 12 plants in group C stayed the same. 3 plants in group C died. |

While you are doing your experiment, precise observation and measurement are essential. To make exact measurements, be sure that any instruments you use are balanced and calibrated. If possible, use metrics when recording your data.

Scientifically, a quantitative analysis based on exact measurements is more exact than a qualitative analysis that relies on observation. For example, "Oct 14-soil sample A weighed twice as much as soil sample B" is considered a qualitative analysis, because it doesn't give the weight of each sample. "Group A, kept in the dark room, ate between 8 and 10 cc per day, and group B, kept in the lighted room, ate between 4 and 6 cc per day," is an example of quantitative analysis, based on exact measurement. It is far more accurate than "more food was eaten by the group in the light."

If you are using scales, rulers, vessels, or other items that measure weight, size, or volume, choose those that can show the smallest differences. For example, a ruler that shows ¹/₁₆" will give you more accurate measurements than one that only shows ¼". "A little less than a millimeter," cannot be precisely compared to a quantity that is "almost a millimeter."

Record Keeping

While you're doing the experiment, *immediately* record your results every time you make an observation. This may be the most important thing you'll do during the project. If you wait a few minutes, you might forget exactly what you saw or what calculations you made. A few hours later, you may begin to interpret what you observed, changing a quantitative analysis to a qualitative one. Even a photographic memory is no substitute for recorded measurements.

Use logs to record everything that happens during your project, and use tables to help you document the data you gather. To make it as easy as possible, design a table *before* you even begin your experiment. Then, you can concentrate on doing the experiment and measuring the results without worrying about how to keep track of the information.

Your table form should include a place for the date of each entry, and whatever measurements and observations you make at the time. Also, leave a final column for notes or comments. This will come in handy if anything unusual happens, which might require a detailed explanation. If you have a control group and one or more experimental groups, you may need a separate table for each group, which will help you to accurately record the information for each group.

In Sabrina's project that tested batteries, she followed her procedures exactly. Only one unexpected result occurred-that the bulbs in the flashlights burned out before the batteries quit. Whenever that happened, she turned off the other flashlights, to make sure that she wasn't giving the other experimental groups an unfair advantage.

Time in minutes			
	Duracell	**Energizer**	**Radio Shack**
5/9	114	114	114
	160	160	160
	25	25	25
5/10	9	9	9
	55	55	55
5/11	25	25	25
5/13	24	24	24
5/14	124	124	124

table continues

Time in minutes (continued)

	Duracell	Energizer	Radio Shack
	26	26	26
	24	24	24
5/15	755	755	755
5/16	66	66	66
	20	20	20
5/17	1517	1517	1517
	0	246	246
	0	82	0
	2944	3272	3190

In the wind turbine project, Theresa used a fairly simple log to record her observations during the experiment. Because she did the experiment over a short period, and tested one model at a time, this worked well for her project.

Model	Electricity Produced	Observations
Four blades with round tips made from - aluminum soda cans, with $1/2$- inserts between blades	None	Turned shaft, but produced no electricity
Four two-inch blades and one-inch inserts, made from aluminum cans	None	Turned shaft, but produced no electricity
Three two-inch blades and no inserts, made from aluminum cans. Blades were bent slightly outward.	$1/2$-1 volt	Blade spun very fast. This model produced the best results
Two blades with tapered but ends and no inserts, made from aluminum cans.	$1/2$-1 volt	Blade turned quickly was slower to start than the three-blade model.
Six blades with rounded edges and no inserts, made from aluminum cans. Two blades were 1 inch wide and bent slightly outward, and four blades were $3/4$ inch wide.	None	Propeller was slow.

Besides having quite a large list of materials and procedures, Theresa's observations were quite extensive on her desalination project. In fact, each of the three methods was almost a mini-project in itself. The entire experiment was conducted over a two-month period, but Theresa tested the distillation method separately, since this was the most complicated to set up and perform. The freezing method, for the most part, took care of itself. Once she determined how to do the boiling method, that, too, was fairly simple to do.

Method	Date	Observation
Distillation	2/18	Started to produce distilled water, but had problems with model.
	3/9	Installed Plexiglas lid on the still, which worked better than previous model. Produced 5 oz. of fresh water from 14 oz. of seawater.
	3/10	Measured salt from yesterday's trial—got 5 teaspoons of salt.
	3/25	Produced 3 oz. of fresh water and 3 teaspoons of salt from 14 oz. of seawater.
	3/27	Produced 2 oz. of fresh water and small (unmeasurable) amount of salt from 4 oz. of seawater.
Freezing	4/14	Produced 4 oz. of fresh water. Salt still frozen with ice.
Boiling	4/15	All water evaporated.
	4/18	Changed apparatus to double boiler. After fresh water cooled down, had $4\frac{1}{2}$ teaspoons salt and 2 teaspoons fresh water.

While you're doing the experiment and recording the data, don't forget to maintain your project log. This is a good place to show any information that can't be recorded on your table, such as locating a graphing program or conversations you've had with teachers or advisors. Include any new research material you've found, or perhaps new discoveries you've made. If you have any problems during the project, you may need to change your procedures. Document these changes, either descriptively or by using photographs, illustrations, sketches, charts, or graphs.

In Theresa Bishop's projects, she documented some of the changes to her models (as well as the models that she eliminated from the experiment) in her procedures and her experimental logs.

If All Else Fails...

For most of you, the experiment will go according to plan and you'll keep your logs current and accurate, to show how your experiment is going. However, if things go poorly, consider changing your procedures or altering your hypothesis. If you started early enough and budgeted your time, you may even be able to change your topic if that becomes necessary.

As we already saw, Theresa Bishop experienced some false starts with both of her experiments. In the wind turbine project, two of the propeller models were too small and light to turn the shaft and produce any electricity, so both models were eliminated from the experimental procedures.

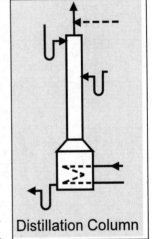

Distillation Column

For the desalination project, the original still, which was built using wood, did not perform well. The water soaked into the wood, and the glue began to melt, which caused leakage, making it almost impossible to measure any results. To fix this problem, Theresa replaced the wood with Plexiglas, which created a better still. She also ran into problems with the boiling method. When she was boiling the seawater in a single pan, the heat caused almost all the water to evaporate, making it impossible to produce any fresh water. She modified her design by using a double boiler, placing a small pan into a larger pan, and placing it on end to collect the fresh water that was produced. The moral of the story? There's more than one way to skin a cat, and if you use your imagination, you can figure out how to change your experiment and save an otherwise good project from extinction.

Before you change or abandon your project, *please discuss it with your teacher or advisor.* She or he may realize that if you "hang in there" a little longer, the experiment will produce results. On the other hand, the teacher may see that by "not getting any results," you are disproving your hypothesis, which is equally valuable.

However, if you cannot salvage your experiment, your teacher may able to guide you toward an alternate project, which can use some of your background research and the materials. In any event, you don't need to go it alone! If you've done your work and tried your best (your research, tables and logs will give ample evidence of that), there's always plenty of help available to you.

Whatever happens, don't try to "fudge" your observations or measurements. Even if your experiment is completely disproving your hypothesis, or, worse yet, doing nothing at all, your project is valuable. For example, one student's experiment on dental adhesives "didn't work." After all the research and preparation, absolutely nothing happened. Because he "guessed wrong," he felt that the project was unsuccessful and he would receive a poor grade. However, because the experiment was well planned and his records were thorough, the project received a good grade, and the student learned some important lessons about science.

Helpful Hint	Did you learn something that may have made your experiment better? You may have found next year's science project!

Remember that "nothing happening" *is* a result. Your experiment may show that the variable has little or no effect on the subject. Although this did not prove your original hypothesis, your experiment is equally valid. Disproving the hypothesis is as important as proving it.

Rather than entirely disproving your theory, the experiment may prove to be inconclusive. This may indicate that the variable was applied in the wrong quantity, strength, or temperature, or that further testing is required. However, the silver lining behind the cloud is that you now have a built-in science project topic for next year!

➤ **In Conclusion...**

Do I have a detailed set of procedures?

Have I designed an experimental log to help me keep track of what happens during the experiment?

Do I have all the materials that I need, including measuring tools?

Am I doing my experiment on a regular basis?

Have I been keeping up my log?

Do I need to change my procedures? (If your answer is yes, make sure that you revise the written procedure list that you created at the beginning of the experiment.)

Is the experiment going poorly? Do I need help or advice?

Chapter 6

Stating Your Results and Drawing Your Conclusions

After the experiment is finished, it's time to look at your results and form your conclusions; in other words, did you prove your hypothesis?

Results

The results of a science project are what happened during the experiment. These are simply the facts—you're reporting what actually occurred. At this time, don't draw any conclusions—all you'll be doing is gathering, organizing, graphing, and charting the material to make the results as clear and meaningful as possible.

First of all, the results are the information you recorded during the experiment. Don't combine or analyze the information, just record your observations without any interpretation or opinion. This is really the hard part! You don't want to draw premature conclusions, but you want to be alert to any trends that you see.

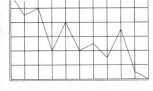

If you wish, you can show the results by creating tables and graphs for each of your variable and control group(s), extending over the life of the experiment.

To see what your data means, you need to combine the data for all of your experimental and control groups. For example, if your pro-

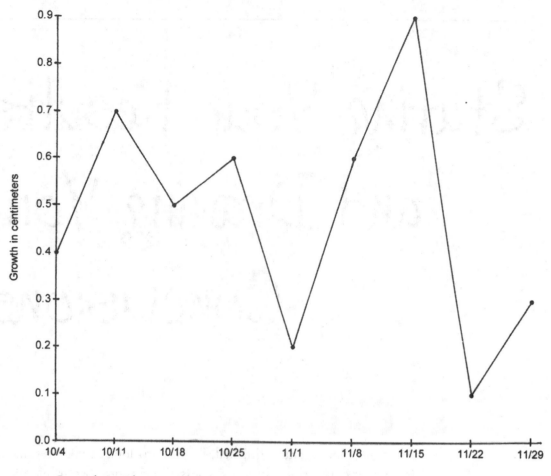

Growth in Plants with No Drainage

ject examined one control and two experimental groups, whose measurements were recorded daily, you will need to look at the data over the life of the project.

The best ways to show your results in a clear, accurate, and visually appealing way are charts and graphs. Line and bar graphs are the most common types of graphs used to present science projects. You can use several graphs or tables, as long as they include all the experimental and control groups. You may also need to make some calculations, such as averages, totals, percentages, or other calculations to make your results meaningful. At the bottom of each table or graph, you can also write one or two short paragraphs that summarize the data and explain briefly what the facts and numbers show.

Computer Tip

A spreadsheet program can be useful in making any calculations that you need. It also will have some built-in functions, such as average, maximum, minimum, or standard deviation, which will make your life easier.

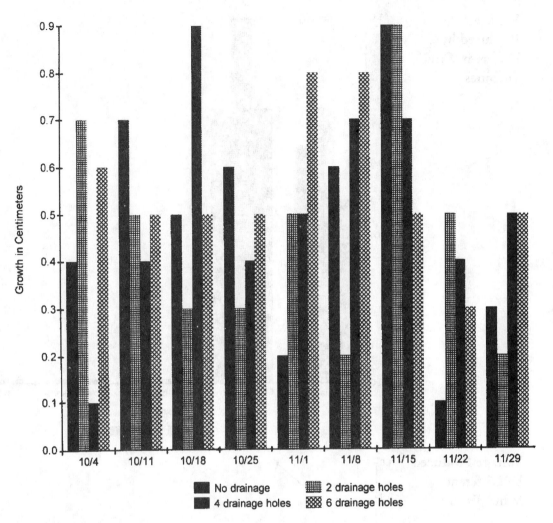

Growth in Plants with Different Drainage

For Theresa's Wind Turbines project, the table shown here summarizes the results of the experiment with the five different models that she built.

Model	Trial 1	Trial 2	Trial 3
2 blades	0.5	0.75	0.65
3 blades	0.75	1	0.75
4 blades	0.01	0.01	0.01
4 blades with inserts	0.01	0.01	0.01
6 blades	0.01	0.01	0.01

However, the same results, displayed on a graph, are even more meaningful.

As you can see from these two examples, although both the bar graph and the line graph accurately show the same results, the bar

**Voltage
Produced by
Different Wind
Turbines**

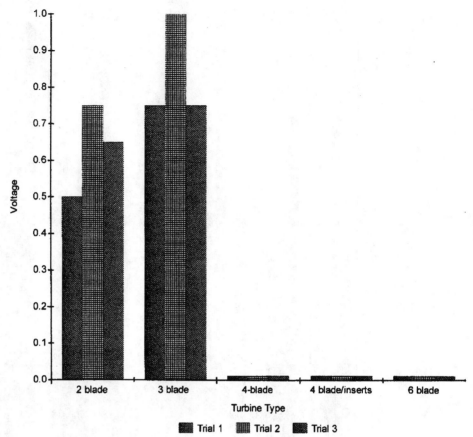

**Voltage Produced
by Different
Wind Turbines**

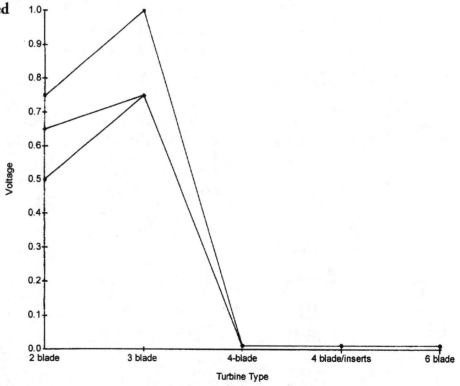

graph more clearly shows the differences between the different propeller models.

For the Desalination project, tables and graphs also helped to display the results of the experiment in a meaningful way.

	Freshwater	**Salt**
Distillation	14	1.0625
Freezing	4	0.01
Boiling	0.25	0.5625

in ounces

A 3-D bar graph showed these results well, even when displaying the fact that no salt could be measured with the freezing method.

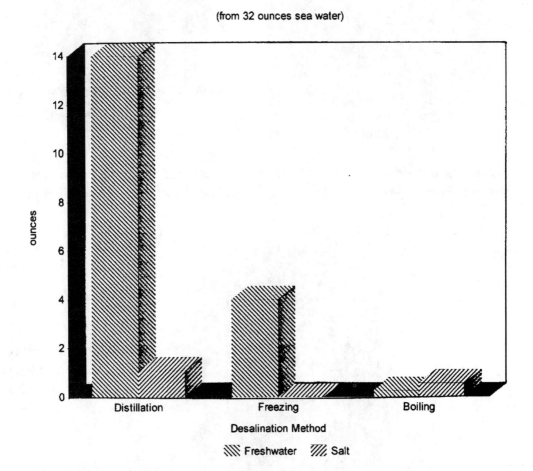

Fresh Water and Salt Produced Using Different Methods of Desalination

Following are three pie charts that show the percentage of fresh water and salt that Theresa got from each fresh water sample. As you will see, however, the pie chart for the freezing method is not all that effective and reflects the difficulty that Theresa had in measuring the salt, which was frozen with the ice.

The objective when using graphs is to combine as much as possible on one graph to show the correlation of data without a loss of clarity. You can use color or design to clearly show the results from each group that you used in your experiment.

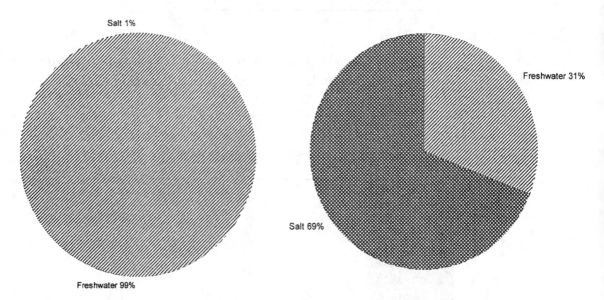

Percentage of Salt to Freshwater Yielded with the Freezing Method

Percentage of Salt to Freshwater Yielded with the Boiling Method

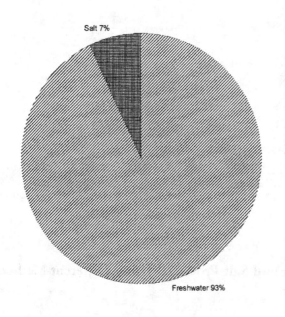

Percentage of Salt to Freshwater Yielded with the Distillation Method

Title each graph or chart, and describe the data being analyzed and compared. Clearly and accurately label each axis, column, or row, including the unit of measurement used. For examples of labeling, review the graphs shown earlier in this chapter.

If you like working with graphs and your data lends itself to this method of presenting results, you might combine several graphing techniques. Remember, however, that as attractive as they are, graphs can only enhance the results; they will not make up for any problems with the experiment.

Computer Tip

If you're using a spreadsheet, a click of the mouse can turn columns of figures into a graph. Some software will let you experiment with the different types of graphs, to see which one you like best.

To help show your results, you can also use any photographs you took during the experiment. This can be a great way to illustrate what happened during experiments that were conducted over several weeks, for example, in a project using plants, where the changes occur slowly over a period of time.

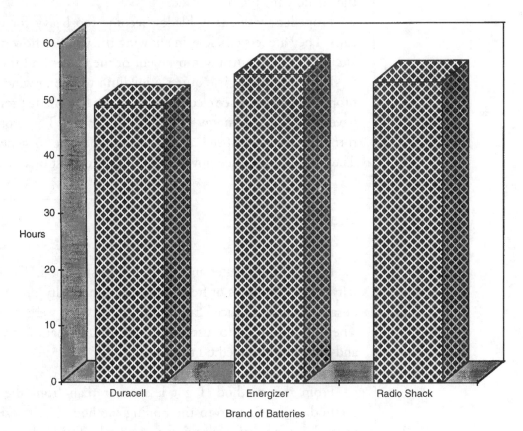

Battery Life. (D size batteries)

In Sabrina Glenn's project on batteries, a graph wouldn't be useful in showing her day-to-day results, since they were the same until the final day, when the batteries gave out, one by one. However, she was able to graph the total minutes for each battery, as shown here.

Besides the tables and graphs, you'll need to write up your results, including a statement of your observations and measurements. Describe how you got your results by explaining any statistical work you've done. Hold on just a little longer—don't draw your conclusions yet. This short statement should clearly and simply explain what happened and what the results showed.

Examples of the results statements from Theresa's two projects are shown here.

Wind Turbines

A two or three blade propeller will produce the most electricity. This is because they can be made large enough to capture the most wind energy possible without being too heavy. The blades can be tapered and turned outward to capture the wind without disturbing the air flow for the next blade.

Propellers with many blades become too heavy for the wind to turn. They are less efficient in allowing the wind to flow past and create the necessary turning movement of the blades and the shaft.

I also discovered it requires a medium to strong wind to turn the propellers and produce electricity. Even the best made propellers must have enough wind energy to produce electricity. The propellers must turn at a constant speed all the time to be able to generate power. They will not produce power if they turn too fast or too slow.

Desalination

Distillation

I got the most water and salt out of this method. The water tasted salty; I got 14 ounces of fresh water that tasted salty, and 8½ teaspoons of salt. The salt produced came in big chunks that were all clustered up. The salt was starting to rust on the pan. I found that this was the easiest and most effective method that I did.

Freezing

From this method, I got less water than from the distillation method, more than from the boiling method. The freezing method yielded 4 ounces of fresh water and no salt. The fresh water was salty and it was difficult to see the salt crystals on the ice. I didn't know what to scrape off.

Boiling

I got the least amount of water from this method, but it was the best tasting water. This water didn't taste salty. I got 2 teaspoons of fresh water and 4½ teaspoons of salt. The salt was very soft and powdery. It was hard to keep the steam from coming out of the sides of the pan.

Sabrina Glenn's project results were quite conclusive.

Battery Life

The Duracell battery lasted 49 hours and 4 minutes. The Energizer battery lasted 54 hours and 32 minutes. The Radio Shack battery lasted 53 hours and 10 minutes.

Conclusions

You may wonder, "how do conclusions differ from results?" Your results show what happened in your experiment, including any necessary mathematical or statistical interpretations, and data correlation. To illustrate the data and make it easier to understand, you've also created charts, tables, and graphs.

To draw your conclusion, look for patterns in the data. Take a close look at your tables, graphs, and charts to see if there's a clear trend. The most important thing is to review your results critically and without bias in order reach a definitive conclusion—a hypothesis is simply an educated guess, and disproving it is as scientifically valid as conclusive proof.

Another possible reason for inconclusive results is a flaw in the project.

The experiment on dental adhesives hypothesized that the bond would weaken in various substances that were high in sugar. With one exception, the bonds didn't weaken at all. He may have been unable to prove the hypothesis because the trials were not carried on long enough or the pull to loosen the bond was too weak.

Write up the project conclusions in a few paragraphs or a short paper, depending on your teacher's requirements. The conclusions will interpret the data and compare the results to the hypothesis. Here, you'll also analyze your own project techniques and procedures, describing how they affected the results and conclusions. Begin your conclusion by restating your question or hypothesis. Next, compare the results to your hypothesis. The data may absolutely prove your theory to be true or false, or the results may be inconclusive. Inconclusive results usually mean that although there may be a trend in your data, it is not strong enough to prove or disprove your hypothesis.

When you write up your conclusions, use your research as well as your results to explain the conclusions reached. The best way to do this is to discuss each fact or occurrence separately. Finally, write a summary that restates the hypothesis and conclusion as supported by the results.

The conclusion from the batteries project is:

My hypothesis was correct, because the Energizer battery outlasted the Duracell and Radio Shack batteries. However, although the Radio Shack battery had the shortest life, it was also the cheapest, so it turned out to be the best buy.

The cost per minute for each battery is shown here.

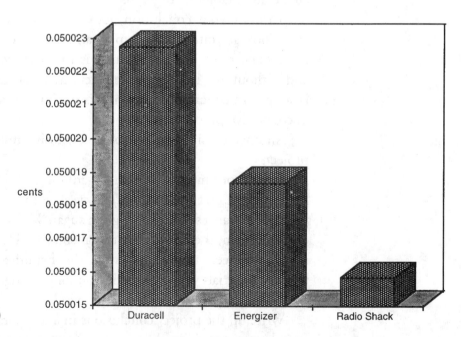

Battery Life.
(cost per minute of use)

Here are the conclusions from the wind turbine project:

> My hypothesis was not correct. I thought the more blades a propeller had the faster it would go. It turned out that fewer blades on a propeller made the propeller lighter and more aerodynamic.
>
> My results were affected by the different materials used and the different sizes and shapes for my propellers. I also found that I had to use a larger fan than I expected in order to get a reading on the galvanometer.
>
> I learned that the propellers have to go at a constant speed to produce energy. I learned that the most aerodynamic propellers are lightweight and have either two or three blades. In Palm Springs, I saw fields of two and three blade propellers. I also learned that these wind turbines are producing electricity right now! I was surprised to see how tall they were and how many different kinds there were.

Here are the conclusions from the desalination project:

> My hypothesis was right; the Distillation method worked the best. The fresh water was still salty, but I got the most salt and water out of this process. However, the Boiling method got the purest fresh water. It hardly had any salt in it. My conclusion is that Distillation got the most water out of the process, but the Boiling method had the best and purest water. The Freezing method didn't work that well—I don't think it was cold enough in the freezer.

Improvements and Enhancements

Whether or not the project proved the hypothesis, you'll need to analyze your experiment. Discuss the strengths and weaknesses of the project procedures. Be honest—there are always some of each! Finally, suggest future changes or improvements.

If this project has inspired you to continue working in this field, briefly state what you plan to do. Even if you're not going to continue, you can speculate on further work that could be done. However, remember that several of the big winners at the International Science and Engineering fairs had been working on variations of the same project for many years, refining and developing their projects. Each year, they built on the strengths and weaknesses of their prior year's experiment.

"Real-Life" Applications

A powerful ending to your conclusions statement is a discussion of any practical value of your experiment. This will show teachers and judges that you can relate your experiment to real-life situations or to other areas. Looking at those types of relationships has brought a great deal of personal satisfaction to many students. For example, a student whose project developed computer systems for the physically challenged took great satisfaction in the contribution the project could make for others. On a more practical level, there is also the possibility for professional recognition (and financial rewards). Some senior-level science project winners have won free trips to the international science fair, cash prizes, and scholarships, and have even been awarded patents.

➤ In Conclusion...

Ask yourself these questions:

Results—have I charted and graphed each of my experimental and control groups? Have I combined the data from all of my groups?

Are my charts labeled and easy to read?

What conclusions did I draw from my results? Did I see any interesting trends?

Have I clearly stated my results and conclusions?

How could I have improved my project?

Can I expand on my project in the future?

Is there any use for this information in the "real world"?

Did I prove my hypothesis? If not, that's OK!

Chapter 7

Building the Project Display

"You never get a second chance to make a first impression" says the expression in many how-to-sell books. Now that you've done your best work on the research, experiment, results, and conclusions, you're ready to present your project. In fact, you are working on an advertising campaign and your "future clients" are the science fair judges. These judges are professors, scientists, engineers, consultants, and business people—in other words, a judge could be anyone with knowledge and experience in your field.

The first objective in advertising is to attract attention, to convince your future customers to take a closer look. Once you've sparked their interest, your prospects will want all the facts they'll need to make their decision. Your tools in this campaign are your science fair notebook and a project display, or backboard.

The Science Fair Notebook

This will contain all your project materials. If you've seen other students' notebooks, you'll realize that this may be a fairly hefty piece of work. However, the good news is that you already have most of the material. You've done the research paper, posed your question and hypothesis, kept your logs, outlined your procedures, and formulated your results and conclusions. All you need to do is edit and revise to get everything into the most attractive and presentable form.

Appearances count, so use an attractive and appropriate cover. Your teacher may have his or her own specific requirements for the size and type of folder, but if not, a good guideline is to use 3-hole, $8\frac{1}{2} \times 11$ paper in a folder or binder

Helpful
Hint

Neatness and legibility count! Whenever possible, type or use computer printout. The professional approach will impress your teacher and science fair judges.

If you're typing, use regular bond paper. Double-space all your written work, with the possible exception of tables, bibliography entries, and footnotes written in standard form, as shown in Chapter 3.

If your teacher allows handwritten notebooks, make sure that your handwriting is completely legible—if you have any doubts, print. Use *ink* only.

The only possible exception is the log section, which represents raw data.

Now, let's review the items to be included in your science fair notebook. Remember that you may not need all of these, depending on whether you're going to be in an International Science and Engineering Fair (ISEF) science fair, and on what your teacher requires.

1. Required Forms
   If you needed any ISEF forms, you must include them in your notebook.

2. Title Page.

3. Table of Contents
   Although this goes right in the beginning of the notebook, it will probably be the last thing you'll create, once the pages are numbered.

4. Abstract
   The abstract is a summary of your project, including the background research paper, the hypothesis, the procedure, and the results. You'll need this if you're filling out an ISEF entry form. If so, limit the abstract to approximately 200 words so that if can fit on the form.

5. Background Research
   Basically, this is the research paper you wrote at the beginning of the project. Now, however, you can polish it to make it look

more professional. Add any comments or suggestions that your teachers made, in order to fix, clarify, and edit your work. You can also include any additional information, such as advice from your teachers or mentors, or new information that appeared in the newspapers or magazines.

6. Bibliography
   This will be the bibliography you submitted with your original research paper. If necessary, update it to include any new sources.

7. Question

8. Hypothesis
   Edit your hypothesis for grammar and spelling. (Do I sound like a broken record? If so, it's because a few too many errors will make you excellent project look unprofessional and badly prepared.) Even if your experiment disproved the hypothesis, *do not change your original theory to fit the results.* Remember that a disproved hypothesis is just as valuable as a proved one.

9. Procedures
   Include a list of all your procedures. If you changed the procedures while doing the experiment, revise them to show how you actually performed the project steps.

10. Materials List
    Include anything and everything you used for your project, regardless of whether you bought, borrowed, or built it.

11. Variables and Controls
    Fully describe each variable and control, and its role in the experiment. Show how you managed and monitored the variables, and how you measured and recorded what happened.

12. Results
    Include raw, smooth, and analyzed data, including all the charts, graphs, tables, photographs, and diagrams. Be sure that all results are neat, legible, and accurately and clearly labeled. Also, describe your observations, which summarize the raw, smooth, and analyzed data.

13. Conclusions
    Edit, spell-check, reread and revise!

14. Acknowledgments
    Now you can thank everyone who has helped with your project. However, don't identify teachers, school, or family by name,

because you're required to remain anonymous when you compete in science fairs.

15. Project Log

This is the only place where neatness doesn't count—you just want to show the detailed progress of your science project, including your diary, working log, notes, and graphs.

Computer Tip

If you're using a word processor, the software can do the page numbering and automatically create the table of contents.

When you've reprinted and collected everything, review the entire notebook. Make sure that the pages are numbered, that you have all the sections in order, and that the pages within each section are in proper sequence. When you're done, have someone review the notebook. After all your hard work, you don't want to be tripped up by pages (or worse yet, entire sections) out of sequence.

The Science Fair Display

The final step is to create your project exhibit. This is your billboard, your TV spot, your glossy magazine page.

Remember, though, that once you've invited the judges to look at your notebook, its contents must live up to the promise of your marketing. Just as with the notebook, the most polished presentation in the world won't substitute for mediocre work.

The purpose of the display is to *summarize* your project. Read that sentence again and remember the key word, *summarize*. Do not try to

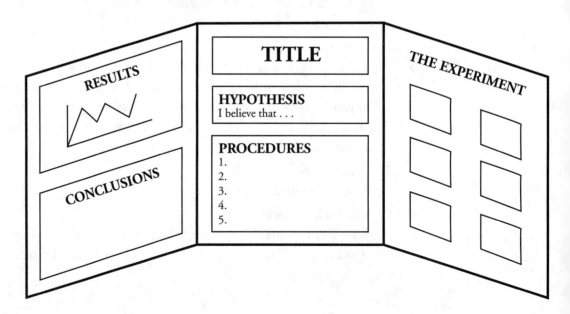

re-create your entire project notebook. Instead, simply cover the main points and the highlights.

Most science project displays are three-sectioned, freestanding backboards. The sections are normally folded or hinged for easier transporting to the science fairs where you'll be competing. However, backboards can have as few as two or as many as five sections to successfully display the material.

You can make your backboards from a variety of materials, from cardboard to Plexiglas. A lot of students use premade backboards, which are commonly made of cardboard or other art materials, and can be bought in many colors. Besides being easier, quicker, and probably cheaper than building your own, a prefab backboard assures that your display will meet exhibit requirements. Another advantage is that you can leave your project display intact in case you want to refer to it again (or in case some author wants to feature it in her book!) If, however, you decide to build your own, use a rigid, durable, fireproof material, such as masonite, pegboard, plywood, or Plexiglas. Although building a backboard will require some time and effort, you can strip off the display materials and use it the next year.

Science fair displays are normally between 3 and 5 feet. When deciding, first check to see if the science fair has size restrictions. Sometimes, you'll see a display that is so large that it cannot be placed on a table and needs to sit on the floor. This happens most often with engineering projects. Be sure to get permission from your local fair officials before designing a floor display. In any event, determine how much material needs to go on the backboard before deciding on the size.

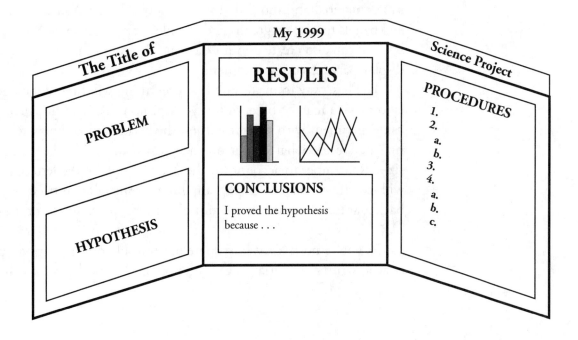

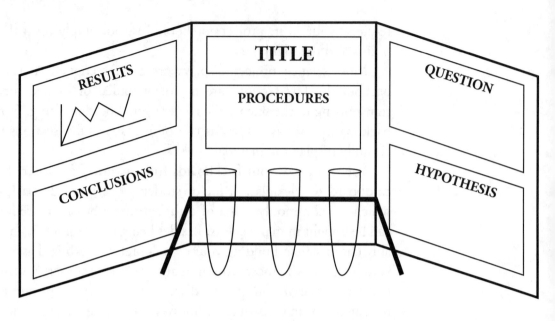

Decide whether you will cover the basic backboard or keep it bare. If you're using pegboard, you may wish to use hooks to attach material. Some students paint their backboards; others glue Velcro strips to the backboard, and attach materials later. If you plan to cover the panels, check the size of the covering material, such as the width of construction paper or self-adhesive papers.

Your display must include a title, the hypothesis, and the procedures, results, and conclusions. You can use all written material, or you can include graphs, photographs, drawings, tables, or other artwork to make the display more attractive. Remember, however, that all this information must fit on your backboard.

Some students have very creatively solved the problem of too much material and too little room on a backboard. You can use several panels to display graphs and samples on the backboard.

You can also create a "mini-diorama" in front of the backboard to display parts of your experiment.

The best way to make sure that everything will fit and look good is to make a map or blueprint of your project display. On paper, you can experiment with what to put on the backboard and how to organize it. Decide what to put on each panel, including the estimated sizes. Remember to account for the size and style of the lettering you will use. If you plan to display anything on the table in front of your backboard, make sure that it won't block an important part of the display.

As you've noticed, at least some portions of your display will consist of written material. The question and hypothesis, which are already short statements, can probably be used without any further editing. However, you can show display printed matter in several ways.

1. Typewritten
2. Computer printout—using word processing, desktop publishing or graphics programs, you can experiment with different sizes and fonts.
3. Hand lettering
4. Stenciling or press-on letters
5. Lettering made on a labeling machine

Be sure to title everything you display, using larger lettering to make it stand out. When doing the written material, the thing to remember is that "less is more." Strive for maximum clarity with a minimum of words. Remember that you are giving a summary. You don't need to show all the facts on the display, because the judges will look at your notebook and interview you to find out more details. Putting too much information on your backboard will make it look busy and difficult to read.

If you include graphs, charts, or tables, create enlarged versions, using color for added interest. If you're not using a computer for graphs and charts, there are several ways to do this. Wide, colored tape can make excellent lines on a graph, and thin, black tape can be used to show gradations. Remember to make the charts, graphs, or tables accurate as well as attractive. If you used computer-generated graphs in your notebook, you may be able to produce larger, colored versions for the backboard.

Photographs or illustrations can be mounted with hinges, corners, or glue. Be sure that anything pasted or glued on your backboard will stay in place for the duration of the exhibit.

A high-quality paper cement is the best way to paste things on a backboard. Be sure to follow the manufacturer's directions, for example, to air the room properly. You could also use staples, nails, pushpins, Velcro, or other methods to attach material.

Plan and coordinate the colors for your display. Contrasting colors that attract attention without being loud or garish usually work well. Metallic colors are good attention-getters, but depending on where your backboard is placed, may reflect glare. Many students have also used colors that enhance the project theme, such as green for botany projects or blue for astronomy or oceanography projects. If you're using several colors, see how they look together before making a final decision.

Always (no exceptions), *always* have extra material on hand. A Sunday night, when the display is due first period on Monday morning, is the worst possible time to find that you've misspelled something on the very last sheet of construction paper. It's a mistake that has often reduced panicked families to rummaging through wastepaper baskets for an even halfway respectable scrap.

Careful planning and measuring, however, will reduce the need for such last-minute resourcefulness. First, plan exactly what you're  going to say and check the spelling of everything to be included. Decide on capitalization and punctuation, and check that for accuracy and completeness, too. Next, see how many lines the text will take. To do this, decide upon the size of lettering you'll use. If you're using computer-generated text, you're ahead of the game. You can print your message in several fonts and sizes to find the one that best suits your display. If you're using another method, you'll need to verify that what you need to say will fit across the panel. If not, you're probably making it too complicated—find an easier way to say it!

If you're buying press-on letters, count how many of each letter, in each size, you'll need for the entire display. Although this may seem like a tedious task, it may save money for buying extra sheets just in case, or, even worse, running out of E's at the last minute. If, however, Murphy's law takes effect, and you run out of letters after the store has closed, remember that with a good eye, a steady hand, a sharp razor blade, and fragments from unused J's and Z's, an F can become an E, a V can be transformed into an A, and an P can be made from a R!

When you're finally ready to place all the material on your backboard, follow these steps for a professional display.

1. Lightly draw lines across the backboard to be sure that your lettering is level

2. Mark the center of each line.

3. Place the center letter(s) of your text on that spot and work outward until you've completed your line. If you're using stencils, you may wish to outline these in pencil and check the line before filling the letters in with marker or paint.

4. If you're gluing things, or using press-ons, keep them lightly attached in case you need to move them.

5. When placing the rest of your written and visual materials, follow similar steps. Lightly mark exactly where each item will go and make sure it creates the effect you really want before firmly attaching it in place.

6. Attach your notebook to the lower left corner of the center panel and the display is done. Open up the backboard, step back, and enjoy. You've done a great job!

➤ In Conclusion..

Have you edited and revised your research paper?

Did you include all the required information in the notebook? (Use the checklist in the science project organizer to make sure.)

Does your display summarize your science project?

Is your backboard attractive and easy to read? Does it meet all the science fair requirements? Is it sturdy and transportable?

Do you want to display anything else (plants, computer, etc.) with your backboard?

Have you attached your notebook to the project display?

Chapter 8

Exhibiting at the Science Fair

The big day is approaching. You've done your best work, you've created an attractive presentation, and you're ready for your first science fair.

Setting Up

On the day before judging, you'll need to set up your display in the exhibit hall. This area can be as simple as a school lunchroom or as elaborate as a civic center or convention hall. Regardless of where the fair is held, however, some things remain the same.

When you enter the exhibit area, officials will check your display for size and you'll be given a location. Projects in the same category are always grouped together. This is for convenience, because there may be different judges for each category. Within a category, places on the exhibit tables are usually assigned in alphabetical order. The only exceptions are oversized displays or those needing electric power. Most science fairs have some fairly stringent safety rules. Here are the basic ISEF rules:

1. If your exhibit produces temperatures greater than 100° C, you must adequately insulate it from its surroundings.
2. You may not display batteries with open-top cells.

3. To prevent accidental contact, you must shield high-voltage equipment with a grounded metal box or cage.

4. Properly shield large vacuum tubes or dangerous ray-generating devices.

5. Place high-voltage wiring, switches, and metal parts well out of reach, with adequate overload safety factors.

6. Electric circuits for 110-volt AC must have a UL approved cord, at least 9 feet long, of the proper load bearing capacity.

7. You must properly insulate all wiring. Do not use nails or uninsulated staples to fasten wiring.

8. You may use bare wire or exposed knife switches only on circuits of 12 volts or less; otherwise, you must use standard enclosed switches.

9. Electric connections in 110-volt circuits must be soldered or fixed under approved connectors. Connecting wires must be properly insulated.

10. Follow the standard safety precautions for chemicals outlined in the booklet *Safety in the High School*. If your teacher doesn't have one, you can get a copy from:

American Chemical Society
Career Publications
1155 16th Street NW
Washington DC 2003336
(202) 872-6168

Installing your project will be easier and quicker if you're prepared. Wear old clothes if setting up involves crawling or climbing. Just in case, have some tools, such as a hammer and nails or a screwdriver, to fix anything that breaks in transport. Also, bring paste or glue to reattach any display material that has become loose or has fallen off. If you use light bulbs that can burn out or glassware that can break, it's a good idea to have extras on hand. If you need an extension cord, pack it together with your other tools. Incidentally, having your own supply kit may make you the most popular person in the hall on setup day.

Don't worry about the safety of your materials. At most fairs, the exhibit area is guarded by professional security personnel. Be assured that everything possible is done to protect your property.

Judging at the Fair

To take some of the stress out of the judging process, it may help to understand what judges are looking for. Although local and state science fairs may be somewhat different, we'll discuss the general process based on ISEF guidelines.

First of all, who are the judges? They're experts in their field from your community, as well as representatives sent by the organizations involved in presenting special awards. ISEF guidelines are specific about what the judges should be evaluating. In speaking to a representative of Science Service (the folks who run the ISEF), she said, "It's no secret. We want the students to know what we're looking for, so that they're better prepared."

The judges will compare all the projects in a single category. Sometimes, if a category has a lot of entries, they may divide it into subcategories. Judges will evaluate the quality of each project, always keeping in mind that it is work done by students, not by professional scientists or engineers.

The most important aspect in judging is showing your knowledge and insight. Although most students have had some help, and some have worked with mentors, you must show that the project is your own work. The judges will also consider whether the project is relevant—a real solution to a real problem and not some outrageous gadget like a device that will automatically walk your dog.

To make the judging process as fair as possible, judges rate projects in the following areas:

- Creative Ability
  The project should show originality in terms of the question, the plan and procedures (including your use of equipment), and the analysis and interpretation of data. They'll probably ask how you got your idea and whether you had any help. You won't be penalized for getting help once you've posed your hypothesis and developed your procedures—that's how professional scientists and engineers work "in the real world."

Warning: A few "don'ts" to keep in mind -- collections and bizarre inventions are NOT usually considered creative.

- Scientific Thought or Engineering Goals
  This is judged differently, depending on whether it is a science or engineering project. For an experiment, the judges will look at your use of the scientific method.

  1. Have you clearly stated the problem?
  2. Was the project at the appropriate level for your age and grade?
  3. Were the procedures well defined?
  4. Have you recognized and defined the project variables and controls (if necessary)?
  5. Did you have a large enough sample?
  6. Did you perform enough trials?
  7. Do you understand the limitations of the data?
  8. Do you understand how your project relates to other research in the field?
  9. Do you have plans for future research, or, if not, have you at least identified what further work is needed in the field?
  10. Have you used scientific literature in your work?

For an engineering or computer programming project, the judges are looking for the identification of the problem and a feasible, practical solution to that problem.

  1. Do you have a clear objective?
  2. Is the objective relevant to the potential users' needs?
  3. Did you develop a "real-life" solution to a "real-life" problem?
  4. Can the solution be successfully incorporated into the design or construction of some end product? (Have you actually created "a better mousetrap"?)
  5. Is your solution an improvement over previous designs?
  6. Have you tested the solution under actual conditions?

- Thoroughness
  How completely did you research the facts, conduct the experiments, and take notes? The judges will check your sample size and the number of tests you conducted if that's relevant to your project. They'll look at your logs and notes, to see if you were a conscientious record-keeper.

- Skill

  The judges will look at the knowledge and abilities you brought to the project, such as laboratory, computational, design, and observational skills. They'll also consider the resources that you had to work with, for example, whether you did your experiment at home, a school laboratory, or a professional or university facility, and the type of equipment and professional assistance that you had available.

- Clarity

  The best ideas will go unnoticed if no one understands them. The judges will want to know that you understand your project. They'll be convinced if you can discuss the project clearly and concisely. (Incidentally, some genuine enthusiasm wouldn't hurt—don't strive so hard to look "professional" that you sound like you've memorized a speech.)

When they look at your display and project notebook, judges will want a clear presentation of the data that *you* have prepared. Although looks aren't everything, keep in mind that the judges will be examining the exhibits before they get a chance to meet and talk with you. Therefore, try to make your exhibit as attractive, clear, and self-explanatory as possible.

Remember that judging is a *comparative* process, which may put your very excellent project behind several others that the judges considered better. If you can, figure out what the winners did to get the recognition that their projects earned. Maybe they did more thorough research, kept better records, or (rarely) made a more impressive presentation. After all, learning some techniques is not a lack of creativity—it's a show of initiative, a quality that will always be well judged!

Be Prepared

Now that you know what judging is all about, you're probably still nervous. You know your project is good and your display is attractive, and you even know what judges are looking for. While you set up, you may have seen some other projects in your category, and you may feel that everyone else's project is better than yours. Don't panic—opening night jitters are normal. However, a bit of common-sense preparation may make it a little less stressful.

- Be well. Get enough sleep the night before judging day and eat a good meal before the judging.

- Look well. You don't need to wear expensive clothes on judging day, but neat, conservative clothes help create a positive image.
- Act well. Don't eat, chew gum, clutch a soft drink, or slouch when the judges are walking through the exhibit area.

- Speak well, both verbally and nonverbally. Smile and be upbeat. Although your project is being evaluated, not your manners or appearance, the judges are only human. They'd rather spend time with an agreeable exhibitor than an unpleasant one.

Take the interview time as an opportunity to discuss your work with professionals in your field of interest. If someone asks a question, don't wave your arm and say "it's all here on the backboard." The judge already knows that. He or she wants to hear you express yourself. Review your notebook the night before so that you'll have the information at your fingertips. Here are some questions that are commonly asked:

- How or why did you get interested in the topic?
- Are there any aspects of the experiment or research that you might have changed or corrected, if you had had the time?
- Do you intend to continue work in this area? If so, how? If not, why not?
- What practical applications or future use does your work have in "the real world"?
- Have you seen the article last month in the Gazette by Dr. So-and-so dealing with the further implications of etcetera and so forth?

Helpful
Hint

Don't be afraid to admit that you don't know an answer or that you haven't read the article or book. You'll make a far better impression with your honesty than by trying to fool an expert.

Science fair judges agree that the factors that come across most positively are knowledge and enthusiasm. A student who chooses a topic that requires a minimum amount of work is unlikely to rate high marks, even if he or she has a beautiful display. However, someone who has really worked to learn as much as possible and has made an effort to follow good scientific procedures will impress the judges, even if the experiment has not worked out well. As we've all heard before, enthusiasm is contagious. Participants who are excited about their experiment and research show that they've gained the true benefit of doing a project and being in a science fair.

When interview is over, smile, shake hands, and thank the judge. When he or she has moved on to the next backboard, you can breathe a sigh of relief. Now it's only a few more hours until you find out if you've won an award and the chance to advance to the next level.

Whether or not you get an award, you're the winner, before you even get to the awards ceremony. In fact, you've been a winner from the moment you made the commitment to do a science project, decided to do your best, stuck with it through the difficult times, and showed your flexibility in considering "alternate plan B" when your experiment seemed to be failing. Your creativity, curiosity and talents have won you new knowledge and confidence, and perhaps even a lifelong enthusiasm.

However, awards are nice, and there are lots to go around! There are usually a wide variety of awards. There are the awards of the particular science fair itself, which consist of first, second, and third place in each category, and sweepstakes winners, who have the best overall projects. Finally, various private companies, research institutes, and military representatives give awards to projects that enhance knowledge in their particular area.

Meet Me at the Fair

Once the excitement and tension of judging and awards night is over, enjoy yourself. Most science fairs go on for several days, to allow both school children and the public at large the opportunity to review the projects.

If you like meeting and talking with people, this might be fun, especially if you have the kind of project that generates many questions. Some exhibitors even prepare handouts describing their work to give out to interested viewers. Most students I've spoken to, especially first-time participants, have spoken with pride of meeting a relative or family friend who didn't even know they were in the fair.

You'll also get the chance to look at others' projects. For comparison, interest, or perhaps ideas on future projects, most participants enjoy looking at others' work. Many students, who wish that they got feedback from the judging process, use this time to look at the award-winning projects in their category.

Finally, in many cities, museums, hospitals, universities, and other institutions join together to congratulate and celebrate the participants in their local science fair. In San Diego California, the fair is held in Balboa Park, the site of most of the city's museums. For the duration of the fair, an exhibitor badge gains the student free admission to any museum. There are also lectures and guided tours, especially for participants. The University observatory, a behind-the-scenes look at the zoo, or a trip to a medical center can be fun and informative. Counseling sessions, given by professionals to advise students about various scientific careers, may be available.

You'll need to keep your project on exhibit until the specified end of the fair. This is to ensure that each student will check out his or her own project when the fair is over.

If you've won an award, congratulations! We hope it's the first of many. If you didn't get a prize, don't let your disappointment spoil the science fair for you or dampen your enthusiasm for future competition. What you've come away with is a working knowledge of the scientific method, an insight into an area of science, confidence in your abilities, and knowledge of yourself.

➤ In Conclusion...

Are you well rested and alert?

Are you prepared on setup day?

Does your display meet all size and safety requirements?

Have you reviewed what the judges are looking for?

Do you know your project thoroughly? Are you prepared to answer the judge's questions?

Have you taken the opportunity to look at other participants' displays?

Have you taken advantage of everything the science fair has to offer?

Did you learn about science and about you?

Did You Have Fun?

Congratulations!!   You did it!!!

Appendix A
Science Project Organizer

Sometimes, organizing a large project can be a huge task. Where should you begin? This science project organizer was designed to help you to get started!

Use the forms included here to help you keep track of everything you'll need and to make sure that you don't forget anything. The best way to use the forms is to make copies of them so that you can have as many copies as you need. The forms are not meant to restrict your creativity, but to allow you to do your project without worrying about the details. If you have a computer, you can actually re-create the forms on your computer and keep track of your project electronically. Finally, you may be able to use the final copies of some of the forms (for example, Using the Scientific Method, or Observations), as part of your science project notebook. Here are some hints on using the forms to their best advantage.

Project Idea Worksheet

When you've come up with a few project ideas, fill out a sheet for each one. This will give you a clear picture of whether you have all the information, help, and materials that you will need.

Sources of Information

You've already started this list on the Project Idea Worksheet, but here you can get more specific about exactly where you will find the fact that you'll need.

Taking Notes

You may find that this is a helpful guide on how to take notes, especially if you haven't done much research before!

Bibliography Worksheet

If you fill this out for each source that you use, as you use it, doing your bibliography will be a piece of cake.

Using the Scientific Method

Here's the place to state all the elements that you'll be using in your experiment. You may want to change the form to fit your individual project (if you aren't using a control group, for example). This sheet, adapted to your experiment, can even be included in the project notebook.

Project Schedule

Filling in your due dates in advance can help keep the project on track—but any calendar or date book will do the trick.

Procedures

List, in advance, all the steps that you'll be doing. If you change your procedures during the project, you might wind up with a "before" and "after" version of the procedures.

Observations

This form will help you keep track of what you see and measure each time you do your experiment—in other words, your experimental log. However, you may want to change this to fit your own experiment, for example, to track how many experimental groups you're using.

Results and Conclusions

Just a handy spot to write a draft of your results and conclusions statements.

Project Notebook Checklist

This may be a handy way to make sure that you've included everything that you need. Remember that depending on where you're exhibiting your project, you may not have to include all these items.

Project Idea Worksheet

Project Idea:		
Sources of Information		
Mentors		
Materials	Source	Costs

Sources of Information

Libraries

➤ _____

➤ _____

➤ _____

Research Facilities

➤ _____

➤ _____

➤ _____

Universities

➤ _____

➤ _____

➤ _____

Government Publications

➤ _____

➤ _____

➤ _____

Businesses

➤ _____

➤ _____

➤ _____

Interviews

➤ _____

➤ _____

➤ _____

The Internet

∞ _____

∞ _____

∞ _____

Taking Notes

Name the source. Include all the information you'll need to identify the source in a bibliography: name of the publication, title of the chapter or article, author, publisher, and date of publication.

Write a summary. What are the main ideas or opinions discussed? If possible, use key words and phrases from the source in your summary sentence.

List the important details. Identify specific details and data that support the main ideas. When you include the exact words of the author or another speaker, use quotation marks to identify the beginning and end of the text.

Bibliography Worksheet

Author	Title	Publisher	City	Year

Using the Scientific Method

Question:			
Hypothesis:			
Experimental Groups	Control Group	Variables	Controls
1.		Experimental:	1.
2.			2.
3.			3.
4.		Measured:	4.
5.			5.

Project Schedule

Date Due	Activity	Date Complete

Procedures

Observations

Date	Experimental Groups				Control Group

Results and Conclusions

Results

Conclusions

Project Notebook Checklist

	ISEF Forms. *Your teacher will be able to get these for you if they are required.*
	Title Page
	Table of Contents
	Abstract. *This is a summary of your project, including background research. If you are preparing an ISEF entry form, this will need to be about 200 words, in order to fit.*
	Background Research Paper. *You can add any new material or insights you've gotten. Also, if you wish, you can revise the paper to make it look more polished and professional.*
	Bibliography. *If you added any new material, be sure to include new sources of information.*
	Problem or Question
	Hypothesis. *The theory that you tried to prove with your project. Remember, do not change the hypothesis to fit the results. An unproven hypothesis is just as valid as a proven hypothesis.*
	Materials. *List all material that you used for your experiment. If you built anything, describe how you made it.*
	Procedures. *Sequentially, list all the steps that you actually followed while doing your experiment, even if they are different from your original procedures list.*
	Variables and Controls. *Describe the experimental groups, control groups, and variables that you used.*
	Results. *Include raw, smooth, and analyzed data, including all graphs, charts, photographs, and diagrams. Your project log can be included here, to show your observations during the course of the experiment.*
	Conclusions. *Did you prove or disprove the hypothesis? How? Why?*
	Acknowledgments. *"Thanks to my mom, my dad, my brother Mike, Aunt Patricia, and my teacher, Mr. Stuart, for all their help and support."*

Appendix B
ISEF Project Categories

Behavioral And Social Sciences

Psychology, sociology, anthropology, archaeology, ethnology, ethnology, linguistics, animal behavior (learned or instinctive), learning, perception, urban problems, reading problems, public opinion surveys, educational testing, etc.

Biochemistry

Molecular biology, molecular genetics, enzymes, photosynthesis, blood chemistry, protein chemistry, food chemistry, hormones, etc.

Botany

Agriculture, agronomy, horticulture, forestry, plant biorhythms, plant anatomy, plant taxonomy, plant physiology, plant pathology, plant genetics, hydroponics, algology, mycology, etc.

Chemistry

Physical chemistry, organic chemistry (other than biochemistry), inorganic chemistry, materials, plastics, fuels, pesticides, metallurgy, soil chemistry, etc.

Computer Science

New developments in hardware or software, information systems, computer systems organization, computer methodologies and data (including structures, encryption, coding and information theory).

Earth And Space Sciences

Geology, geophysics, physical oceanography, meteorology, atmospheric physics, seismology, petroleum, geography, speleology, mineralogy, topography, optical astronomy, radioastronomy, astrophysics, etc.

Engineering

Civil, mechanical, aeronautical, chemical, electrical, photographic, sound, automotive, marine, heating and refrigerating, transportation, environmental engineering, power transmission and generation, electronics, communications, architecture, bioengineering, lasers, etc.

Environmental Sciences

Pollution (air, water, land), pollution sources and their control, waste disposal, impact studies, environmental alteration (heat, light, irrigation, erosion, etc.), ecology, etc.

Mathematics

Calculus, geometry, abstract algebra, number theory, statistics, complex analysis, probability, topology, logic, operations research, and other topics in pure and applied mathematics.

Medicine And Health

Medicine, dentistry, pharmacology, veterinary medicine, pathology, ophthalmology, nutrition, sanitation, pediatrics, dermatology, allergies, speech and hearing, optometry, etc.

Microbiology

Bacteriology, virology, protozoology, fungal and bacterial genetics, yeast, etc.

Physics

Solid state, optics, acoustics, particle, nuclear, atomic, plasma, superconductivity, fluid and gas dynamics, thermodynamics, semiconductors, magnetism, quantum mechanics, biophysics, etc.

Zoology

Animal genetics, ornithology, ichthyology, herpetology, entomology, animal ecology, anatomy, paleontology, cellular physiology, animal biorhythms, animal husbandry, cytology, histology, animal physiology, neurophysiology, invertebrate biology, etc.

Category Interpretations

Following are project areas about which questions frequently arise. This list is included only to provide some basis for interpretation of the category descriptions.

Instruments

The design and construction of a telescope, bubble chamber, laser, or other instrument would be engineering if the design and construction were the primary purpose of the project. If a telescope were constructed, data gathered using the telescope, and an analysis presented, the project would be placed in Earth and Space Sciences.

Marine Biology

Behavioral and Social Sciences (schooling of fish), Botany (marine algae), Zoology (sea urchins), or Environmental Sciences (plant and animal life of sea, river, pond).

Fossils

Botany (prehistoric plants), Chemistry (chemical composition of fossil shells), Earth and Space Sciences (geological ages), and Zoology (prehistoric animals).

Rockets

Chemistry (rocket fuels), Earth and Space Sciences (use of a rocket as a vehicle for meteorological instruments), Engineering (design of a rocket), or Physics (computing rocket trajectories). A project on the effects of rocket acceleration on mice would go in Medicine and Health.

Genetics

Biochemistry (studies of DNA), Botany (hybridization), Microbiology (genetics of bacteria), or Zoology (fruit flies).

Vitamins

Biochemistry (how the body deals with vitamins), Chemistry (analysis), and Medicine and Health (effects of vitamin deficiencies).

Crystallography

Chemistry (crystal composition), Mathematics (symmetry), and Physics (lattice structure).

Speech And Hearing

Behavioral and Social Sciences (reading problems), Engineering (hearing aids), Medicine and Health (speech defects), Physics (sound), Zoology (structure of the ear).

Radioactivity

Biochemistry, Botany, Medicine and Health, and Zoology could all involve the use of tracers. Earth and Space Sciences or Physics could involve the measurement of radioactivity. Engineering could involve design and construction of detection instruments.

Space-Related Projects

Note that many projects involving "space" do not go into Earth and Space Sciences but in Botany (effects of zero G on plants), Medicine and Health (effects of G on human beings), or Engineering (development of closed environmental system for space capsule), etc.

Computers

If a computer is used as an instrument, the project should be considered for assignment to the area of basic science on which the project focuses. For example, if the computer is used to calculate rocket trajectories, the project would be assigned to Physics; if the computer is used to calculate estimates of heat generated from a specified inorganic chemical reaction, the project would be entered in Chemistry; if the computer is used as a teaching aid, the project would be entered in Behavioral and Social Sciences.

Glossary

abstract

A short summary of the main points of a project. This is normally between 200 and 250 words in length.

clip art

Pictures that are included with many word processing, graphics, and desktop publishing software. These pictures can be added to your documents and can sometimes be modified using graphics software.

conclusion

Interpretation based on results and answering the question or comparison suggested by purpose.

control group

Identical to the experimental group, except that no variables are applied. This represents the test group that has all variables standardized and forms the basis for comparison.

controls

Factors that are not to be changed. *Do not* confuse with *control group*.

data base

Data files organized so that they can be manipulated and accessed in a variety of groups and sequences. Working with a data base requires specialized software

dependent variable

The factor that changes as a result of altering the independent variable. Also, the change in events or results linked and controlled by another factor that has also been changed.

desktop publisher

A system that performs printing functions, such as page layout and composition. A desktop publisher can incorporate files from many sources, such as spreadsheets, word processors, and graphics and photo processing programs.

experiment

A planned investigation to determine the outcome that would arise from changing a variable or from changing "natural" conditions.

experimental group

A group of subjects to which independent or experimental variables are applied.

experimental variable

See independent variable.

graphs

Illustrated form of presenting raw, smooth, or analyzed data.

hypothesis

States what the experimenter believes will happen as a result of the experiment.

independent variable

The item, quantity, or condition that is altered to observe what will happen; something that can be changed in an experiment without causing a change in other variables.

interpretation

One's personal viewpoint based on the data. This can be based on either qualitative or quantitative analysis, and may become a part of the project's conclusion.

materials

All items used in the course of the experiment.

measured variable

See dependent variable.

observation

What one sees in the course of the experiment. Observations are often incorporated into raw data.

procedures

Steps that must be followed to perform an experiment.

qualitative analysis
Analysis made subjectively, without measurement.

quantitative analysis
Analysis made objectively, with measurement devices.

question (or problem)
The basis of the hypothesis or objective of the experiment.

research
The process of learning facts or prior theories on a subject by reviewing existing sources of information.

results
The observations made during an experiment and the analysis of the data collected. Results can be shown in graphs and tables.

scientific method
Manner of conducting an experiment, using valid subjects, variables, and controls, and accurately recording results.

spreadsheet
A program that manipulates data laid out in columns and rows that contain cells of data. A spreadsheet can perform mathematical functions on the data and automatically recalculate results when any of the data changes. A spreadsheet program can also create a variety of graphs based on the data.

tables
Written form of presenting raw, smooth, or analyzed data.

variable
A condition that is changed to test the hypothesis or a condition that changes as a result of testing the hypothesis.

word processor
Software that allows you to create and edit written documents, including the ability to insert, delete, and change text, change fonts, lay out tables, and print a variety of paper sizes on different printers.

Index

About the Author

Maxine Iritz is a software developer and the author of several popular children's science books, including *Blue Ribbon Science Fair Projects* and *Super Science Fair Sourcebook*.